The
SILVER-
PLATED
AGE

BARD

Tom B. Jones

II

Coronado Press

First printing: 1962
Second printing: 1964
Third printing (type reset): 1971
Fourth printing: 1973
Fifth printing: 1977
Sixth printing: 1979

ISBN 0−87291−018−0

Manufactured in the USA

Contents

Preface

SOMETIMES EVEN PROFESSORS like to write just for fun, and that was the way *The Silver-Plated Age* began. After the manuscript had won a McKnight Foundation Humanities Award for 1960, however, it appeared that this material might be of some interest to general readers and students.

This little book is concerned with the intellectual life of the Roman Empire, mainly in the period of the Good Emperors in the second century A. D. Baldly stated, its thesis is that the illiberal liberal education then in vogue stultified the intellect and thus contributed to the marked decline of creativity that signaled the end of ancient civilization. To be more specific, those who went through the sequence of the schools of grammatistic, grammar, and rhetoric were provided with a standardized education that gave all students the same kind of training and furnished them with the same frame of reference. Within this frame of reference people could communicate intelligibly with one another; and, from the purely literary point of view, a liberal education in the best sense was acquired. On the other hand, the system was defective in that the curriculum was one that had crystallized in the Hellenistic Age centuries earlier; it was oriented toward the past and tended to ignore the present. In the Roman imperial period, when a host of new problems needed fresh viewpoints for their solution, the educational system deadened men's minds with its uniformity of training and its exaltation of the authority of antiquity.

After graduation from the school of rhetoric, some students went on to professional training in law or medicine or pursued the formal study of philosophy. Into each of these fields they tended to bring the methods and attitudes acquired in their earlier training. This was conducive neither to creativity nor originality, for the schools had stressed book learning. In science or medicine, therefore, much of the research that was subsequently undertaken involved a sampling of the opinions of the ancient authors rather than a careful program of observation and experiment. Much too often, when a person determined to discover "something new," he concentrated on the reading of obscure authors of the past and so picked the brains of the dead instead of exercising his own.

(7)

⊕

Since this book is not intended for the instruction of learned colleagues, the chapters which follow have a minimum number of footnotes, but additional citations and references will be found in the Supplementary Notes at the end of the last chapter. In these notes, too, appear brief identifications of the ancient authors which are merely to serve as a guide for the general reader who may also wish to consult the *Oxford Classical Dictionary* or some comparable reference work.

Permission to quote from the *Loeb Classical Library* translations of certain ancient authors (Aulus Gellius, Fronto, Epictetus, Celsus, Philostratus, Plutarch, and the Greek Anthology) has been graciously accorded by the Harvard University Press. Quotations from A. O. Prickard, *Longinus On the Sublime* and A. Gwynn, *Roman Education* are given by permission of the Clarendon Press, Oxford; those from A. J. Brock, *Greek Medicine,* by permission of E. P. Dutton & Co., New York. Likewise, the Egypt Exploration Society has allowed me to quote from *P. Oxy.* 2407. Exact citation and acknowledgement are given below in the footnotes.

Tom B. Jones

1

Pax Romana

If a man were called upon to fix the period in the history of the world, during which the condition of the human race was most happy and prosperous, he would, without hesitation, name that which elapsed from the death of Domitian to the accession of Commodus.

Edward Gibbon

I, Dionysius, lie here, sixty years old. I am of Tarsus; I never married, and I wish my father never had.

Greek Anthology

AELIUS ARISTIDES, a famous Greek orator who visited Rome during the reign of the pious Antoninus, declared that the Roman Empire was Utopia itself. Peace and prosperity without precedent had been established through the agency of the Romans who had brought the art of government to its highest point. Under a monarchy without tyranny the subjects of the emperor enjoyed social and judicial equality, the major benefits of democracy, yet they were spared the disadvantages and inconvenience of political participation. Consequently, the whole world was in holiday in this golden age. Civilization had been brought to remote places; the whole traverse of the sun was Roman property. People everywhere clung to Rome, and the very thought of secession was abhorrent to them. As he looked about the city of Rome, Aristides concluded that those who lived in the imperial capital were the most fortunate of all. Rome was huge; its size and even its name symbolized the strength of the empire. Everything in the world could be seen in this great metropolis, and thus its inhabitants (like the later Bostonians) had no need to travel.

Dio Chrysostom, another prominent orator of the second century A. D., told the emperor Trajan that the best of all possible worlds, one well-ordered by the judgement and virtue of a single good man, had been achieved. It was a fine thing, the younger Pliny thought, that one person should be willing and able to shoulder the responsibility of providing for the common good. According to Plutarch, the world was so peaceful that there was no need for statesmanship; war had

(9)

vanished, and the people had as much liberty as was good for them. The emperor Nerva, said Tacitus, had reconciled the two incompatibles, liberty and the principate. Even Epictetus, who seldom found perfection anywhere, was forced to admit that the emperor had established a profound peace: there was no war, no brigandage, no piracy; a man could travel to any part of the empire without fear of molestation.

Now it has been said of Aristides that his speeches were occasionally distinguished by their wealth of words and poverty of fact. Moreover, Tacitus, in some passages of his historical works, has been suspected of irony. Perhaps some allowance should be made for the fact that Dio was addressing Trajan when he praised the principate, or that Pliny produced a panegyric on the same emperor. Epictetus, as will soon appear, qualified his remarks on the benefits of Roman rule, while the comments of Plutarch, on second thought, might admit of more than one interpretation.

On the other hand, although he must test his sources with care, the historian knows that human nature is perverse: people usually look for Utopia in the past or in the future; they seldom discover it in the present. Perhaps the contemporaries of Aristides lacked his keen perception. We shall see that many of them did not recognize, or refused to admit, their good fortune. If Aristides was right, and they were wrong, these critics and complainers resembled the Lydian in Dio's story who, because he had no trouble, went out and bought some.[1] Epictetus, for example, after enumerating the benefactions of the imperial régime, had the ingratitude to complain that Caesar could not protect man from fire, shipwreck, earthquake, lightning, or emotional distress. So unappreciative was Epictetus that he advocated withdrawal from the public into a private Utopia where each man should create a solitude and call it peace. Aristides must also have been unaware of the attitude of his contemporaries in Alexandria, for at that very time they were busily engaged in maligning their good Good Emperors in a series of accounts which glorified an imaginary Alexandrian resistance to an equally imaginary imperial tyranny.[2] As for the city of Rome, Juvenal did not share Aristides' impressions of its attractiveness, while Dio found that in all the great urban centers of the empire the condition of the proletariat was truly desperate. In fact, most people of this time were so far from discerning the felicity of their age that a Lucian could prosper by scoffing at it, and there was a large and growing religious sect whose members were not only disloyal and even subversive but also looked forward to an escape from the Roman Empire into the Kingdom of Heaven.

In his praise of Rome Aristides stressed the value of its commerce
and the robust health of its economy, and archaeology, too, bears
witness to the widespread and voluminous trade of the empire in the
first and second centuries A. D. The products of one province have
frequently come to light within the environs of another. Roman
artifacts, particularly the coins of gold or silver, have been discovered in
countries beyond the limits of the imperial frontiers. The expanding
economy of some provinces was impressive. The Gallic provinces, for
example, had developed the manufacture of textiles and pottery as well
as the production of wine. Once, they had imported these things from
Italy; now, the Gauls were not only self-sufficient but were also
exporters, while the Italians, having lost their trade, needed governmental subsidies to keep their heads above water. Foreign trade was so
brisk that there began to be a shortage of silver coin within the empire,
but this deficiency did not stem entirely from the great demand of
India or Germany for Roman silver: the busy Roman miners had
exhausted many of the mines, and times were so peaceful that the great
booty which Rome had once acquired by foreign conquest was no
longer a regular source of income. In the unhappy days of the Republic
Julius Caesar had brought back so much gold from his victories in Gaul
that the price of that precious metal at Rome had fallen to an
unprecedented low. The Dacian conquests of Trajan and his return with
the treasure of Decebalus temporarily relieved a money shortage at
Rome which had been building up for several generations. Nevertheless,
the problem was recurrent: at one point in the reign of Marcus
Aurelius, imperial funds ran so low that the philosopher emperor held a
public auction in the Forum and disposed of personal possessions in
order to finance military operations on the Danubian frontier;
fortunately, these campaigns produced enough loot for Marcus to
repurchase his property. During the reign of Commodus, the money
situation continued to deteriorate and reached a crisis in the closing
years of the second century.

Archaeology also confirms the allusions of Aristides to the extreme
urbanization of his age and the innumerable building projects intended
to enhance the appearance of the towns; in Africa, Gaul, Greece, Asia
Minor, everywhere, every place was full of "gymnasia, fountains,
gateways, temples, shops, and schools." Unlike Athens, every city had
not the imperial gifts or the private philanthropy of an Herodes Atticus
with which to beautify itself without running into debt. When Trajan
sent his treasury expert, or economist as we would call him today, to
the hard-pressed cities of Bithynia, the imperial trouble-shooter found
plenty to do. Trajan's expert was, of course, the younger Pliny whose

reports to his superior are most revealing. At Prusa Pliny found the city finances in chaos; and the Prusenses also needed a public bath — probably in more ways than one. Nicomedia had no fire department. Both Nicomedia and Sinope had grown to the point where the water supply was insufficient; old aqueducts must be repaired or new ones built. At Nicaea ten million sesterces had been spent without result on the construction of a theatre, and a poorly designed gymnasium, although its walls were more than twenty feet thick, was not sufficiently well built so that anyone dared to put a roof on it. At nearby Claudiopolis the people had chosen a swampy site where they were "sinking, for I cannot call it building," a big public bath.

Financial troubles were not the only ones which plagued the towns, for there were violent inter- and intra-city quarrels that raged continuously. Aristides, who came from Asia Minor and was in the thick of politics at Smyrna, cannot have been ignorant of the discord, yet he painted a glowing picture of provincial and civic harmony. Dio Chrysostom of Prusa tried manfully to reconcile the warring factions everywhere. More than a dozen of his orations were addressed to the citizens of the Asianic towns — Prusa, Nicaea, Nicomedia, Apamea, Tarsus — and he tried to reason with the turbulent Alexandrians of Egypt, but to no avail. At Tarsus the good people greeted his efforts with what must have been the ancient counterpart of the Bronx cheer; at least, "snort" does not seem to be the best translation of the Greek word.[3] At home in Prusa a hostile faction tried to ruin Dio with a charge of treason against the emperor.[4] Plutarch attempted in a less vigorous way to discourage squabbling on the local level; it was all a tempest in a teapot, he argued, and simply not worthwhile.

The civic bickering described by Dio, Pliny, and Plutarch went on for centuries. A newly published papyrus of the third century A. D. contains the minutes of a public meeting in Oxyrhynchus. The document reads in part:

> The members of the first tribe cried: "Yes, noble syndic! You have administered well!"
> The members of the second tribe cried: "... You have acted unfairly!"
> Nemesianus: "This ought not to have been done today..."
> Menelaus, syndic: "Well, I only wanted to give equality to the tribes..."
> Nemesianus: "I have already certified that this ought not to have happened today."
> Menelaus: "Well, I made provision for this in the minutes..."

Nemesianus: "I have already certified."

Menelaus: "What sort of people, then, do you want to take part in the meetings?"

The assembly cried: "Those about to become of age...."

Nemesianus: "This should not have taken place today."

Menelaus: "Do not disturb the assembly."

Nemesianus: "Do not set pitfalls for the assembly."

Heron, son of Euhemerus: "Let them all take part in the meetings."

Menelaus: "....and if your credit is good....enrol them."

Nemesianus: "If my credit is good, it is no thanks to you."

Menelaus: "and it is no thanks to you if mine is....do not confuse the assembly...."

Heron: "You are the one who confuses everything."[5]

Perhaps another of Aristides' observations also deserves investigation, for he says: "....viewing the senate....you would think there is no truer aristocracy than this." It is possible, of course, that the senate had improved since Pliny's day a generation earlier, but two of his letters which describe senatorial procedure are not easy to forget. By the end of the first century A.D., the election of the magistrates had long been the prerogative of the senate rather than a function of the *comitia*. As time passed, the ceremony of election became less and less dignified: Pliny said that the senators were behaving worse than any popular assembly, for there was no regularity in speaking, no respectful silence; the candidates milled about with their patrons in "a most indecent confusion." The custom of balloting *viva voce* seemed to lie at the root of the trouble, and it was therefore decided to adopt a secret written ballot. Pliny wondered how this would work; by the time of his second letter he had the answer. Instead of writing soberly the names of the preferred candidates on the ballots, some senators scribbled "pleasantries," even some very naughty things. Pliny was shocked but not completely surprised; he noted sadly that the emperor had now another excuse for taking over functions that should have been exercised by the senators.

Near the end of his oration Aristides once more returned to his vision of a new golden age. He criticized Hesiod as no prophet for having terminated his descending series of periods — golden, silver, heroic — with an Age of Iron. The progression had not ended there as Hesiod had supposed it would. The curve had shot upward again: the unhappy iron men had now perished in their turn and were succeeded by a race of gold. A quite dissimilar concept of the second century, however, had been formulated by Aristides' contemporary, the historian Florus. The story of the Roman people, said Florus, might be likened to the life of man: the Romans had passed from childhood under the early kings to adolescence under the Republic, manhood in the time of Augustus, and old age shortly after that. Florus seems to have doubted whether the temporary revival under Trajan was more than a second childhood.

Enough has been said to suggest that the opinions of Aristides were not shared by all of his contemporaries and may even have been faulty in some respects. To judge from its external appearance, the second century seemed flourishing enough. The Roman Empire attained its greatest territorial extent; the peak of urbanization for any period of antiquity was reached; literacy was never more widespread in ancient times, trade never more far flung, or the bourgeoisie more numerous. Yet, criticism and pessimism were rampant; people were uneasy about the present and feared the future. It was a strange period — uncomfortably like our own in many ways.

⊕

There is no dearth of literary sources for the era of Roman Peace. In fact, no other period of antiquity presents a comparable wealth of material for study. Although the Pax Romana begins with Nerva and ends with Marcus Aurelius, it is helpful to try to pick up the threads of the story in the reign of Nero and to seek the epilogue in the early years of the third century. The works of more than three score authors survive from this crucial century and a half. Many of these writers were truly prolific: we have eight of Dio's discourses; the essays of Plutarch are still more numerous, even excluding the *Lives*: Galen and Lucian are not far behind; Aelian, Pliny the Elder, and Aulus Gellius were encyclopaedists. To begin with Petronius and Seneca and run the gamut to Cassius Dio, Diogenes Laertius, and the early Philostrati involves more than a little reading, but at least the chore is tempered by variety: Arrian's *Discourses of Epictetus,* the *Institutes* of Quintilian, Chariton's *Chaireas and Callirrhoe,* the *Satires* of Juvenal, Longinus *On the Sublime,* Ptolemy's *Almagest,* the *Life of Apollonius of Tyana* by Philostratus. This is the age of Tacitus, Suetonius, Martial, and Apuleius. Pausanias wrote his guidebook to the cities of Greece; there is a textbook of Roman law by Gaius; poetically inclined Isaac Waltons may read the *Halieutica* of Oppian. The names of Lucan, Persius, Statius, and Frontinus are familiar enough, but Polyaenus, Nicomachus, and Favorinus are definitely off the beaten track — not to mention Sextus Empiricus.

These authors were seldom objective about the age in which they lived; and, of course, some of them ignored it altogether. Few made even a show of impartiality; some were openly tendentious. Some were purposedly untruthful; others would not have recognized the truth if they had happened to find it. They do not tell us everything about their age, but their works do reveal facets of it rather fully.

Much has been written about the Pax Romana. Its governmental system, society, literature, art, religions, law, economics, scholarship, thought, science, and technology have been made the subject of many scholarly treatises.[6] There are biographies of the Good Emperors and of their famous contemporaries.[7] However, the last word on the subject may never be said, partly because new facts constantly come to light, and partly because the period can be approached from many different points of view. Just as the so-called Fall of Rome has been a matter for lively discussion over the centuries, so the Roman Peace will continue to stimulate the curiosity of generations to come.

In the muddled middle of the twentieth century A.D., the problems of the second century can be viewed with sympathy. The Romans of that bygone age worried about over-urbanization, recalcitrant teenagers, public finance, and even the problems of the aged. Their artists and literary men were struggling to discover new and appropriate forms of expression. Busy people, who could not do much reading, liked condensations and epitomes: the *Attic Nights* of Aulus Gellius was the *Readers' Digest* of the second century. Citizens expected their government to provide them with all kinds of social services and then complained about high taxes. Workers dreamed of a six-hour day.[8]

Like our own age, the second century with its foibles invited satire – and got it from experts. After scrambling and crawling through the literary underbrush of the Pax Romana, it becomes increasingly difficult to take its authors and their period very seriously, and some readers may be distressed to find that no concerted attempt has been made to do so in the pages which follow.

FOOTNOTES

1. Dio, *Forty-third Discourse*, 1.
2. The so-called Acta Alexandrinorum, collected in H. A. Musurillo, *Acts of the Pagan Martyrs*, Oxford 1954.
3. Dio, *Thirty-third Discourse*, 32 ff.
4. Pliny the Younger, *Letters*, X, 8.
5. E. Lobel, C. H. Roberts, E. G. Turner, and J. Barns, *Oxyrhynchus Papyri*, Vol. XXIV (London 1957), no. 2407. Reprinted by permission of the Egypt Exploration Society.

6. See the Bibliography, but by way of example here: M. Hammond, *The Antonine Monarchy* in *Papers and Monographs of the American Academy in Rome*, Vol. XIX, Rome 1959; C. G. Starr, *Civilization and the Caesars*, Ithaca 1954; L.Friedländer, *Darstellungen aus der Sittengeschichte Roms*, 4 vols., Leipsig 1921-22; J. W. Duff, *Literary History of Rome*, Vol. II (rev. ed.), London 1959; J. M. C. Toynbee, *The Hadrianic School*, Cambridge, Eng. 1934; T. Frank, ed., *Economic Survey of Ancient Rome*, 5 vols., Baltimore 1933-40; J. Beujeu, *La Religion romaine à l'apogée de l'Empire*, Paris 1955; H.–I. Marrou, *History of Education in Antiquity*, London 1956; F. Schulz, *History of Roman Legal Science*, Oxford 1946; S. Dill, *Roman Society from Nero to Marcus Aurelius*, Oxford 1928.

7. B. W. Henderson, *Life and Principate of the Emperor Hadrian*, London 1923; E. E. Bryant, *Reign of Antoninus Pius*, Cambridge, Eng. 1895; A. S. L. Farquharson, *Marcus Aurelius*, Oxford 1951; F. A. Lepper, *Trajan's Parthian War*, Oxford 1948; P. L. Strack, *Untersuchungen zur römischen Reichsprägung des zweiten Jahrhunderts*, 3 vols., Stuttgart 1931-37; H. von Arnim, *Leben und Werke des Dio von Prusa*, Berlin 1898; A. Boulanger, *Aelius Aristide*, Paris 1923; F. Della Corte, *Suetonio*, Milan 1958; R. Syme, *Tacitus*, 2 vols., Oxford 1958; M. Yourcenar, *Memoirs of Hadrian*, New York 1954; S. Perowne, *Hadrian*, London 1960.

8. Greek Anthology, *Hortatory Epigrams*, no. 43.

2

A Familiar Crisis

Learning's a treasure — and a trade never starves.

Trimalchio

The roots of education are bitter, but the fruit is sweet.

Diogenes Laertius

HISTORY WILL SHOW that the Pax Romana and the Eirene Amerikane had at least one thing in common: a crisis in education. The uneducated educator is not indigenous to North America, nor did the species first evolve in the twentieth century A.D. Although Dio's audience has shrunk perceptibly in the last eighteen hundred years, about the same generous portion of ancient and modern readers would probably brand as atavistic his claim that there is more to education than lyre-playing and wrestling.[1] It is interesting and instructive, yet discouraging to discover that in the days of the Second Sophistic, just as in our own time, people were arguing about what to teach and how to teach it.

The great debate over education which raged during the first two centuries of the principate was occasioned by an expansion of educational facilities which was in turn a byproduct of widespread prosperity. Many new schools were established throughout the empire; Juvenal laughed that even Thule was seeking a rhetorician. The imperial government, municipal authorities, and private philanthropy all contributed to the expansion of the schools. The Flavians and the Good Emperors, big cities and little towns, and public-spirited citizens like Pliny the Younger not only made possible an increase in the number of teaching establishments but also raised the salaries of teachers to an eminently respectable level. Although universal education was not attained, literacy was never higher in antiquity than in this period.

Unfortunately, educational expansion was accompanied by a watering-down of subject matter and a general lowering of standards. There were not enough good teachers to go around, and there was a tendency to depress the level of instruction to a point where the mediocre student would be accommodated. Most people accepted the prestige value of a formal education, but its quality was not a matter of

(17)

universal concern. A poor education was deemed better than none at all, and, in the long view, the difference between good and poor seemed very slight. Such chronic cynicism and downright ignorance, when combined with the idea that schooling is for children and adolescents only, has never done the cause of education much good.

The decay of education was recognized and bitterly criticized by a number of writers who flourished in the late first and early second centuries A.D. despite minor differences of opinion, the critics agreed on basic issues. They found the contemporary system of education unsatisfactory, and they blamed students, teachers, and parents for it. The critics had similar schemes for improvement; they also agreed among themselves on the ideal curriculum and its content.

Quintilian, Tacitus, Dio, Plutarch, and Lucian were unanimous in their belief that a proper education should make men virtuous and wise and thoughtful, able to receive communications from their fellows and in turn to communicate intelligibly with them. The ideal education was wide and thorough; it began early and continued until the end of a man's life. Seneca said that a man should keep learning as long as he is ignorant, or, in other words, as long as he lives. People should try to comprehend the wisdom of the past, but mere archaism and antiquarianism were condemned as unimaginative pedantry. It was desirable to progress and to find new things, but these men freely acknowledged their debt to their ancestors. They realized that, just as a child learns from his parents, so too the experience of the human race might serve as teacher to the present. The novel was not to be confused with the new, and, while slavish imitation was to be discouraged, the virtue of good models was fully appreciated since they taught one to distinguish the superior from the mediocre.

The importance of an education was never in doubt. As Marcus Aurelius observed, "a man should spend liberally on education," while Plutarch maintained that "people should make nothing of greater concern than the education of their children." There was a belief that most children could be educated regardless of social position or family background. In Plutarch's opinion, "indifference ruins a good natural endowment, but instruction amends a poor one." Quintilian was also optimistic, for he said: "Among children there is a shining promise of many accomplishments." Then he added, "When that dies out as they grow older, it is plain that it was not talent that failed, but training."

The debate, then, was not over an extension of education to the lower classes. Under fire were the method and content of contemporary education, and on these points the critics had much to say. They advocated a return to an older system which they believed to be efficacious. The counter-arguments of the "progressives" are unknown, but their methods are revealed by the specific criticisms of the traditionalists and by the reforms which these critics advocated.

Nature, reason, and habit were the basic words in Plutarch's educational creed.[2] Nature meant natural endowment, reason was learning, and habit was constant practice and the real keystone. Quintilian, Tacitus, and Diogenes Laertius concurred that ability, instruction, and practice were fundamental. Ability must be present in the individual himself, for "the best husbandman cannot improve soil of no fertility"; in instruction, it was essential to employ the most competent men at all levels since the "most skillful teacher can teach best the little things as well as the great ones"; all else depended on practice "which will soon increase our ability."

A general education which would give a broad knowledge of many things was a primary objective. As Tacitus remarked, a man of learning was like a warrior taking the field in full armor. Vitruvius had long ago enumerated the many fields of knowledge in which an architect must be versed, and Quintilian recommended the same wide study for the perfect orator. Plutarch agreed that education should not be narrow and overspecialized; he wished it to be capped by training in moral philosophy, although physical education was not to be neglected. All the critics emphasized again and again that, although it was essential to be able to speak and write well, one must have something to say; in short, knowledge must come before skill. There was no substitute for hard work and constant application. Too many doctors, said Galen,[3] were like athletes who wanted an Olympic victory but did not want to train for it. The critics agreed with Euclid that there was no royal road to geometry or any other worthwhile subject.

The insistence of the critics on the importance of certain attitudes or procedures suggests that an opposite view was characteristic of the "progressives." Diogenes Laertius said that progress in education was achieved by pressing hard on those in front and not waiting for those behind. Quintilian believed that competition among the students should be fostered; he also felt that, while praise might inspire a student to greater effort, rebuke in some cases might have a similar effect, and therefore he advocated alternating the two. Even more shocking to his opponents must have been his ideas that students could be worked very hard if exposed to a variety of studies and that memorization was absolutely necessary; a good memory was essential to an orator, of course, and it could be developed through training, but Quintilian undoubtedly provoked a flurry of protest when he suggested that the ability to memorize was an indicator of intelligence. The "speak as you please" school of thought was also selected as a target; Quintilian defined usage not as the language of the past, and especially not as the language of the majority, but as the agreed practice of educated men. Apparently some "experimental" teaching of foreign language had come into vogue because Quintilian took a firm stand on the necessity for learning conjugations and declensions from the very beginning of the study. The initial rapid progress claimed for the "experimental" method, he said, was more apparent than real; teachers who used the new method were making the mistake of starting with what should come at the end. For school use, anthologies of literature were universally condemned by the critics; little snippets of this or that author had no teaching value because it was essential to read a work in its entirety. It was Seneca's opinion that:[4]

> You cannot sample the masterpieces of great minds by means of summaries. You must examine the whole, work over the whole. Their structure is a totality . . . . and if any part is removed, the whole may collapse.

Direct denunciations of the current educational inadequacies were common. Tacitus blamed the educational failures of his age on the decay of old-fashioned virtues, the carelessness of parents, the ignorance of teachers, and the laziness of young men. The decay of antique virtue was by this time an equally old-fashioned and empty theme, but there was something to be said for Tacitus' other complaints. It was probably true that the lack of discipline in the home stemmed from the fact that mothers were no longer responsible for the early training of their children. Other critics agreed that fathers and mothers should not delegate educational responsibilities to servants. Even the use of servants would not be so bad, said Plutarch, if they were carefully selected; ordinarily, however, the unemployables were placed in charge of the children, while the most trustworthy slaves were chosen to manage the master's farm, ship, shop, or other business. Parents were also careless about the selection of teachers; proper investigation of their mental and moral qualifications was not made, and very often a teacher would be chosen because he charged a smaller fee than his competitors. Once the child was in school, the parents might interfere in senseless and annoying ways: one teacher wrote a whole book about the wrongs he had suffered from parents.[5]

The critics felt that many instructors did not possess the proper attitudes or adequate qualifications for teaching; Aulus Gellius[6] remembered with asperity an ignorant grammarian of Eleusis. Teachers often competed for students; they tried to attract large groups by lowering standards or substituting spectacular for sound material. In some cases there was an attempt to push the students ahead too rapidly, while in other instances they were coddled and chaperoned far beyond the time when they should have been able to shift for themselves. Many of the school exercises were absurd and did not truly prepare the students for careers in, for example, oratory or law. Some teachers tried to give advanced instruction in fields in which they were not themselves qualified. As Petronius said, some try to teach more than they know. The conservative attitude was expressed by Quintilian who remarked that "a grammarian should be ignorant of some things." Both Plutarch and Lucian charged that the schools had more than their quota of glib lecturers who played to the crowd, phonies who delighted in a display of pretended knowledge and were poseurs *par excellence,* men who strove for novelty at the expense of soundness.

The remarks of the critics about the students suggests that neither students nor critics have changed very much in the last eighteen or nineteen centuries. Dio noted that all men are hard to teach but easy to deceive. Students were difficult; there was no more discipline in school than at home. Their interests were focussed on actors, gladiators, and horseracing. They would listen attentively to gossip or the account of a dinner party or a parade, but they were not so eager to hear what their teachers had to say. Lectures were given and received in the classroom very much as they are now. In Plutarch's wonderfully amusing essay called "On Listening to Lectures" he complains that people learn to talk before learning to listen; this subverted a divine wisdom that had given men two ears but only one tongue. Familiar student types were to be found in the ancient classrooms: the know-it-all who always wanted to show off and argue with the teacher, the eager beaver who nodded his head in agreement with everything and thought it all just superb, the unresponsive character who sat blank and unmoved throughout the whole lecture, and many more. "And so in the particular case of a lecture, not only frowning, a sour face, a roving glance, twisting the body about, and crossing the legs, are unbecoming, but even nodding, whispering to one another, smiling, sleepy yawns, bowing down the head, and all like actions, are culpable and need to be avoided."*7*

Fortunately, the critics were not content merely to enumerate the shortcomings of the educational system; they also had much to offer in the way of constructive advice. Quintilian would not have approved of the private tutoring that Marcus Aurelius received. He felt that it was much better for a boy to go to school. A good teacher could manage several students just as well or even more effectively than one; much of the instruction did not have to be of an individual nature. Of course, too large a group would result in the neglect of the individual, and that should be avoided. Nevertheless, there was much to be said for the social contacts that a school provided; it made possible experiences which would be useful in adulthood and often led to the formation of valuable life-long friendships. There were also opportunities for competition and emulation that would be lacking at home. The argument that contacts made in the schools corrupted the boys could rarely be justified; if the boy had the proper training at home, he would not be led astray in school.

Quintilian was a shrewd judge of students. He knew the limitations of the mimic who would waste his time in horseplay, or those of the quick boy who could learn the easy things swiftly but was undone by his early success and could not keep up when the harder tasks came along. Quintilian much preferred the intelligent, inquiring student who was nevertheless content to be led. He knew also that there were differences in talent and that the teacher must identify them: one boy might show more talent for history, another for poetry, or another for the law; therefore, the teacher had some responsibility for vocational guidance. A school could not be operated on an assembly line basis.

In the learning process, said Quintilian, both listening and reading were important. There was much benefit to be had from hearing a speaker, but reading allowed more careful study; a student could proceed at his own pace, go over the material again and again, and exercise more judgement than when carried along by a speaker and influenced by all the externals of a live performance. Books were as necessary for the student as a set of tools for the farmer. Quintilian and Pliny the Younger,[8] his pupil, stressed the value of translation from Greek into Latin, or vice-versa, as an aid in developing style or the choice of the precise word. Practice in paraphrasing passages from selected authors or in imitating their styles served the same purpose. These exercises contributed to facility of composition. When it came to writing something, Quintilian thought it a mistake to make a rapid draft which would later be revised. It was much better to exercise care from the beginning so that the work could be chiseled into shape rather than fashioned anew. Unlike Dio,[9] who insisted that it was time wasted to read rather than be read to or to write rather than dictate, Quintilian felt that solitude was essential to real thought. Dictation might permit greater speed, but it encouraged the formation of bad habits: the person dictating, for example, might be ashamed to hesitate and thus become careless in composition. Dictation allowed no privacy, yet privacy was necessary for thought as one studied the thoughts of other or prepared to communicate his own ideas.

The critics deplored the narrow, short-range objectives of the ordinary education, and they were not in sympathy with the motives that brought most students into the schools. As Quintilian said, "I would not wish to have even for a reader a man who would compute what monetary returns his studies will bring him." The ideal education was not primarily vocational; it was designed to produce a man of knowledge, capable of logical thought, able to express himself, and, above all, morally strong. Such a man would then be prepared to acquire the more specialized skills of the profession for which his ability and inclination fitted him. Galen[10] believed that a thorough training in scientific logic and demonstration was valuable for his own field of medicine and for many other fields both scientific and humanistic. Grammar, rhetoric, music, mathematics (particularly geometry), astronomy, history, poetry, drama, and philosophy must all be combined to produce an educated man.[11] To the acquisition of knowledge, power of thought, facility of expression, and virtue these subjects could contribute in more ways than one. History, for example, provided models worthy of emulation in its lives of virtuous men as one studied the literary excellence in the style of the great historians. Furthermore, as Cicero had said,[12] "To be ignorant of what happened before you were born is to live the life of a child forever." Poetry also contributed to the growth of morality, knowledge, and style, while philosophy taught logic and virtue.

The better teachers did not aim at producing scholars, but rather they hoped to develop rational human beings. Some felt that the main purpose of study was the cultivation of reason. They knew that the initial phases of advanced studies were difficult, that students needed to be encouraged and even stimulated to ask questions though independent thinking was an ultimate goal. Every good teacher knows that the mind is not a vessel to be filled but a woodpile to be kindled. As Seneca[13] had pointed out, one's primary duty was not to study, but to have studied, for the function of the liberal arts was to prepare the mind for virtue. Students who sought knowledge merely to display it were often criticized by teachers who had higher ends in view.[14] Education was not to read books but to put knowledge into practice, said Epictetus.[15] The art of grammar or the art of music did not possess the power of contemplation. In writing, the art of grammar can be helpful, but it cannot advise you whether to write or not. Only the reasoning faculty can judge with discernment the various arts and their uses. It is of no great consequence to master the received account without forming some opinions of your own. What difference does it make, say Epictetus and Seneca,[16] if one knows what learned men say about this or that if one has not tested the thing for himself?

Although by the second century A.D. there were innumerable treatises on grammar, rhetoric, oratory, philosophy, architecture, music, mathematics, and many other subjects, these works were read mostly by teachers, very advanced students, or persons who had already completed their formal education and wished to continue certain studies privately. While many of these treatises might be called textbooks, they were not used as we use textbooks today; that is, each student was not expected to have a copy of the text for the course. This had two distinct advantages: it sometimes forced the teachers to teach, and it protected the students from a lot of bad writing. Instead of poring over textbooks, the students read and studied works of literature from which they might learn something of the intricacies of style and at the same time undergo an exposure to the "great books" of classical antiquity. As Seneca said,[17] "In choosing a teacher, we may go to the ancients who have unlimited leisure to teach us."

Everyone read, memorized, and recited the greatest of the great books, the *Iliad* of Homer. Here was the master poet whose work could instruct men, it was felt, even in matters other than the art of poetry. Homer topped every list of recommended authors. He should be first, middle, and last, said Dio,[18] for "Homer gives every boy, adult, and old man as much as he can take." Not merely a model for verse-making Homer was, or could be, the model for every species of eloquence sublime in great subjects and decorous in small ones, he was Jupiter himself. Homer had even helped the philosophers to express their ideas,[19] and he was an accredited moralist because he discredited the mean and emphasized the good.

Hesiod was admired for his easy flow of words and his ability to mold a useful maxim in an unforgettable way. Plato taught acute reasoning and possessed an Homeric eloquence; that "remarkable man" was quoted with great frequency by numerous authors. Of all the ancients, it was said, Xenophon alone could satisfy the requirements of a man in public life: the graces themselves had formed his style. Together Plato and Xenophon guided youth onward to learning, leadership, and virtuous conduct. Euripides, too, was useful to a man in public life, for he abounded in fine thoughts and precepts of morality that might have been uttered by the philosophers themselves. Menander was admired for his portrayal of character as well as for his style. The great models for oratory, although their works had other sterling virtues, were Demosthenes and Cicero; Dio praised Demosthenes for the impressiveness of his thought, and Quintilian said that as a philosopher

Cicero rivaled Plato. Other authors recommended as being valuable for style and content were Pindar, Thucydides, Herodotus, Sallust, and Livy.[20]

It is worthwhile noting that some critics of the educational system, no matter how vigorously they urged a return to the supposed methods and standards of earlier times, were not always completely sure that the change would bring about the thorough improvement that they desired. There was occasionally a nagging doubt that the older system might not have been perfect. It was also deemed possible that the general decline which people sensed could not be blamed entirely on an educational failure.

The critics who advocated reform commonly assumed that the traditional framework and curriculum would be maintained, and that better teachers and higher standards would be sufficient to bring education back into line. Petronius, however, once pointed out that Sophocles, Euripides, Pindar, Demosthenes, and Plato had not had the advantages of a formal education. Sextus Empiricus wondered how the blind could lead the blind. The rhetors, for example, who were supposed to teach oratory, were often mute as fish in a court of law. Were the rhetors, as they claimed, like whetstones whose purpose was not to cut but to put the edge on a knife? Sextus thought not. Instead, he recalled a story about Corax, the early Sicilian teacher of oratory, and a pupil of his who appeared in court as rivals in a suit. They outraged the jurors by their antics and were both condemned by a verdict that became a proverb: "a bad egg from a bad crow." What passed for education, said Dio, had little practical value; people had a mistaken notion that the man who had read the most books and knew the most literature was the wisest and best educated person. In the schools of the sophists there were many people growing old in ignorance. All the schoolmasters in the world could not set a city to rights. It is only fair to add that Dio was leading up to the importance and utility of philosophical training, but the concept of philosophy as a panacea had already been pretty well demolished, as every one except the philosophers seemed to realize. Galen,[21] although he admired philosophy, was dubious about philosophers; both he and Lucian were fond of making the point that, since the philosophers could not agree among themselves, they could scarcely be considered to have a stranglehold on knowledge. Plutarch noted sadly that there were philosophers who oversold their product; they advertised for students and then provided no real instruction or advice.[22]

It must have occurred to some critics that the decline of education might be a symptom of some greater disease. National decadence was a favorite theme of the Roman historians. Sallust, Livy, and Tacitus had all lamented "these parlous times." If conditions were as bad as Sallust claimed and then *continued* to deteriorate for another century and a half, as Tacitus claimed, it is truly amazing that the Roman Empire survived as long as it did. Cato had blamed the Greeks for the decline of morals; Sallust and Livy thought the corruption stemmed from the luxury engendered by the empire; Tacitus found his cause in the principate. In any event, contemporary education could not be the root of this trouble.

In Tacitus' *Dialogue on Oratory*, where the decadence of oratory was a subject of discussion, it was admitted that great oratory was born of great causes, of which there was some dearth under the principate. Longinus knew this argument and rejected it.[23] It was not only oratory that was in the doldrums, but there was also a "world-wide barenness of literature." Freedom and democracy might breed noble spirits, said Longinus, but it was common to bewail the present and idealize the past. For his part, he would put the blame on avarice and indolence.

There was more to decadence than a failure to live up to the standards of the past. What distressed the critics, although they were generally inarticulate about it, was a lack of progress. Archaism or imitation were not the answers to the problem of the age. Cicero had been modern in his own day, but he would seem old-fashioned if he had lived in the second century A.D. Tedious in introduction, long-winded in narrative, and wearisome in digression, Cicero would be out of place.[24] Imitation was not sufficient in itself. If the men of antiquity, who lacked models, had been content with what they possessed, there would have been no inventions. If no one had ever accomplished more than the man whom he copied, Roman poetry would not have advanced beyond Livius Andronicus, history would amount to the barest of annals, and painting would consist merely of tracing the outline of a shadow cast by the sun. Whatever is a copy of something else is only a resemblance and therefore inferior to the original. "Must we convict our own age of this unhappy deficiency and consider that at last nothing improves?"[25]

These are the sounds of a dying civilization. They echo down the long corridors of time to activate a sympathetic vibration in the twentieth century. We cannot help the Romans now. There is no need to diagnose or to prescribe when the prognostication already belongs to history, but we may profit from a post mortem.

FOOTNOTES

1. Dio, *Thirteenth Discourse,* 19.
2. Plutarch, *Education of Children,* 4.
3. Galen, *Best Physician is a Philosopher,* I, 1.
4. Seneca, *Epistles,* 33.
5. Suetonius, *On Grammarians,* 9.
6. Aulus Gellius, *Attic Nights,* VIII, 10.
7. Plutarch, *On Listening to Lectures,* 13. Reprinted by permission of the publishers from F. C. Babbitt, *Plutarch's Moralia,* Cambridge, Mass.: Harvard University Press, 1927.
8. Pliny, *Letters,* VII, 9.
9. Dio, *Eighteenth Discourse,* 18.
10. Galen, *On his own Books,* 41 ff.
11. Galen, *Protreptikos,* 39.
12. Cicero, *Orator,* 120.
13. Seneca, *Concerning a happy Life,* IV.
14. Epictetus, *Discourses,* I, 29; III, 23.
15. *Ibid.,* II, 17.
16. *Ibid.,* II, 19, 9; I, 4 and Seneca, *Epistles,* 33.
17. Seneca, *Epistles,* 53.
18. Dio, *Eighteenth Discourse,* 8.
19. Sextus Empiricus, *Against the Grammarians,* 13.
20. For a complete list of authors, see below pp. 36-45.
21. Galen, *On his own Books,* 43.
22. Plutarch, *Precepts of Statecraft,* 51.
23. Longinus, *On the Sublime,* 44.
24. Tacitus, *Dialogues,* 22-23.
25. Quintilian, *Institutes,* X, 2, 4-10.

3

Reading, Writing, and Rhetoric

A grammarian's daughter, having known a man, gave birth to a child which was masculine, feminine, and neuter.

Greek Anthology

EVEN TODAY one could hardly ask for a more perfect training in the liberal arts than the ideal education described by Quintilian and his contemporaries. Unfortunately, this ideal was, and always had been, a dream that did not correspond with reality. It may also be prudent to suspect some exaggeration in the charges of the critics that education under the Pax Romana had taken a turn for the worse, although it is certain that it did not get any better. A lowering of standards would have weakened education, of course, but if the trend by some remote chance had been in the other direction and standards had been raised this would not have removed the most serious defect in second century education. Ordinarily, education is largely a product of, and is responsive to, the civilization in which it exists. This does not seem to have been true during the Second Sophistic when a rigid and outmoded system of education was employed to outfit everyone, regardless of his projected vocation or profession, with the same standardized straight-jacket. Our age is the first to achieve mass production in industry; the second century did it in education. After a description of the educational machine in operation, we shall be prepared to analyze its effect upon the intellectual activities of the graduates from the schools.

The education of classical times has been the subject of a number of books, some good and some bad, but all seem to include the same material.[1] It is safe to assume that the basic outlines of ancient education have already been sketched and that future research is not apt to effect major revision of the picture which we now possess. Consequently, a brief summary of what is known about the school system will suffice for the purpose at hand.

Under the Pax Romana there were two kinds of education: Greek and Roman. The Greek type had been "perfected" in the Hellenistic Age; it was employed in the eastern half of the Roman Empire and consisted of instruction in the Greek language, Greek literature, and other subjects with which the Greeks had concerned themselves for

(29)

some time. The Roman type was really a subtype of the Greek since it covered the same ground and merely added the study of Latin and Latin literature; the higher it advanced from one level of instruction to another, the more Greek it became. This Roman type of education was found in the western provinces, especially in Italy, North Africa, Spain, Gaul, and Britain.

Normally, a child began his education at the age of seven. Accompanied by his paedagogue, he would set off early in the morning for the *schole* or *ludus* where he would endure a daily stint of about six hours of instruction. Reading and writing were the principal skills attained in this "grammatistic" or primary phase of education. The child learned to recognize and to write the letters of the alphabet; from letters he progressed to syllables, and finally to reading and writing words. This was followed by the reading, writing, and reciting of simple maxims which were dictated by the teacher. There was much stress on pronunciation. Quintilian thought that Greek and Latin should be taught simultaneously, but that the first instruction should be in Greek because a Roman child would pick up Latin anyway. Another subject begun in the primary school was arithmetic; its study was sometimes continued beyond that level under special teachers.

By the age of eleven or twelve the child would be ready to study with a "grammarian" who gave instruction not only in grammar but also in literature, history, geometry, music, and even elementary astronomy. Grammar itself, according to Quintilian, consisted of learning about parts of speech, accents, pronunciation, orthography, semantics, and grammatical constructions; in addition, the pupils read and studied standard works of literature and got much practice in oral and written composition. Sextus Empiricus[2] said that grammar had three parts: historical, technical, and special. The first involved instruction concerning gods, persons, and places; this would consist of the explanatory material for the elucidation of the literary works read and studied in the schools. The technical part included the rules relating to elements and parts of speech, orthography, and the Greek idiom. By elements Sextus meant vowels, consonants, syllables, and accents Greek idiom meant "good Greek" without barbarisms or solecisms, and "good Greek" was defined by Sextus, though not by some grammarians, as the common usage of educated persons. The special portion of grammar was devoted to a study of style and usage in poets and prose writers. Sextus was pretty contemptuous — his chronic attitude toward most other writers — of a certain Asclepiades who had divided history into three parts: true (factual), false (fictions and legends), and "as if true" (comedies and mimes). This was absurd, said Sextus, and useless because the grammarians neither taught how to establish historical truth nor how to write history; the latter fell in the province of rhetoric. He was not sure that the special part of grammar had much value, either, for he claimed that the grammarians rated poems on their clarity. Thus, the best poem would be so clear that no explanation would be necessary, while a bad poem would not be worth untangling anyway.

The criticisms of Sextus rarely seem as acute and penetrating as he evidently thought they were. It was inevitable in his blast against the grammarians that he should mention with his usual scorn the name of Dionysius Thrax, the author of a little treatise which was to be the bible of grammarians for many centuries. Sextus quotes the celebrated Thracian as having said that grammar had six parts: skilled reading according to the scansion, explanation concerning the tropes which the poems contained, exposition of the phrases and histories, the discovery of etymologies, the reckoning of analogy, and the judging of compositions. Sextus was quoting directly here the second sentence of Dionysius' famous grammar just as in another place he gave an almost exact quotation of the first sentence: "Grammar is mainly expertness regarding the language of poets and prose writers." Dionysius then went on to define correct reading (anagnosis), pitch, accent, the recital of epic poetry, vowels, consonants, diphthongs, long and short syllables, parts of speech (under which he listed nouns, verbs, adverbs, articles, pronouns, prepositions, adjectives, conjunctions), and so on. The work of Dionysius was soon elaborated and expanded by commentators, and from their writings we sometimes get the illusion of being in the schoolroom and listening to the grammarian lecture:

> Skill is a thing most indispensable to the life of men.... Know then what is the rule, and what is the strength of the rule, and what is the soundness of the rule, for then we may define the art of grammar. For how can we define this if we do not first know the rule? .... Learn then what is knowledge, and what is known, and what is experiment, and thus learn what makes up grammar.

The teacher then goes on to give examples. A thing known is a thing, for example, which is mathematically established: "the perimeter of a circle is *three times* its diameter." Another kind of knowledge is empirical: the knowledge a farmer possesses about farming, and so on.

There are four main divisions of art or skill, says another. These are theoretical, practical, poetic, or mixed. Astronomy, strategy, and dancing are given as illustrations of the first three, while medicine is a mixed skill that combines the theoretical, practical, and poetic — unfortunately for the patients, this mixed skill too often had plenty of the first and third and not enough of the second. A sister skill of medicine is grammar, says the teacher, for grammar is also mixed: when it deals with history, it is theoretical; the practical part is defined as what we would call grammar; and the study of literature, the poetic. Sextus would have hotly denied the claim of the grammarian who said, "Grammar is most useful for rhetoric and philosophy."

The method of studying what Sextus called the technical part of grammar was by drill, both oral and written. In the case of the poets and prose writers, the teacher would read or recite a passage, and the student would then try to imitate his performance. The teacher lectured on various matters pertaining to the text; he elucidated its meaning, explained the mythological, geographical, and historical allusions, corrected the text if necessary, and also made a detailed criticism of the style. Again there was drill in the form of questions and answers: "Who was so-and-so? She was so-and-so's mother."[3] The attention given to practice in speaking might vary with the teacher; some teachers tried to anticipate the rhetorical training which came later. In written composition there were exercises in writing narratives, in paraphrasing, translation from one language into another, and versification.

The study of Latin grammar was very much like that of the Greek. A number of handbooks and other treatises were produced during the first and second centuries A.D. Although Varro, a contemporary of Cicero, had done much to stimulate the study of the Latin language, the foundations for the teaching of Latin grammar were laid by Verrius Flaccus, Pliny the Elder, and Palaemon. These three authors, of course, lived in the first century A.D., and Quintilian seems to have borrowed from all of them in preparing the relevant sections of his *Institutes*.[4]

Since Palaemon was the teacher of Quintilian, it is not surprising that the latter was influenced strongly by him, but Palaemon's *Ars Grammatica* had a wide circulation in the second century as well. It might be noted that the personality of Palaemon, in addition to his scholarship, was long remembered. A former slave, he fought his way to the top of his profession by sheer ability. His facility in extemporaneous speaking and his prodigious memory were greatly admired while his egotism and immorality were notorious in an age when many people displayed more than the usual quantity of both unpleasant traits. Palaemon also had a talent for making money; his annual income was close to three quarters of a million sesterces, half of which came from his teaching and the other half from his estates and from his chair stores which sold ready-made clothes. Palaemon was much too colorful for a grammarian; he was more like the rhetoricians who presided over the schools which were on the next educational step above the schools of grammar.

The age for beginning rhetorical training varied somewhat, but the average entrants were probably about fifteen years old. Rhetoric was essentially training in oratory. There was the usual squabble about whether rhetoric was a power, a habit, a science, or an art, but Quintilian defined it as an art, the art of speaking well. Oratory or rhetoric belonged to what was called the political category of prose; the other two categories were historical (including the three types of Asclepiades mentioned above) and theoretical (philosophical, scientific, technical).[5] Oratory itself was divided into three classes: advisory (symbuleutic), demonstrative (epideictic), and forensic (judicial); Quintilian's corresponding terms would be deliberative, panegyrical, and judicial. The instruction in oratorical preparation and delivery was given under five headings each one of which was regarded as a special study in itself. These were: the discovery and development of material, arrangement of material, verbal expression or style, memorization of speeches, and hypocrisis, or manner of delivery. A large part of Quintilian's *Institutes* is given over to a discussion of this training. The reading and study of authors begun in grammar school was continued, greatly extended, and performed at a much higher level. Written and oral composition, especially the latter, were naturally major activities. Exercises were carefully graded in difficulty. Even before coming to the rhetor, the students would have had practice in turning into prose the versified Aesopic fables; they would have begun short narratives and the composition of *chriae,* or anecdotes about famous persons. With the rhetor, simple encomia, denunciations, descriptions, and discussions of general questions finally led up to the full dress oration complete with proem, epilogue, and all the trappings.

While it was generally conceded that oratory was a useful and necessary study, the rhetorical schools were often criticized for the poor quality of their graduates; it was alleged that the schools encouraged affectations in style and manner, that there was an abundance of theory and a lack of practical training. At best, the discourse of the students was stilted and unnatural. Speeches were sung and danced rather than presented in the proper oratorical manner; Tacitus complained that everything was topsy-turvy, for the actors nowadays danced eloquently while the orators spoke voluptuously. The subects employed for declamation in the *suasoriae* and *controversiae* were frequently criticized as unrealistic. In the *suasoriae,* some course of action might be discussed; in the *controversiae*, propositions would be maintained or denied. Lists of declamation topics have survived, and we must agree that they put some strain on the imagination. One shudders to think what some bright little Roman Teenager would do with such a topic as "Leonidas urged the Lacedaemonians to eat a good lunch, for they would dine in Hades; Asinius accepts the lunch, but declines the dinner." Among other *suasoriae*, there were: *Alexander considers whether he should sail the ocean; the Athenians deliberate the removal of the Persian trophies; Agamemnon deliberates whether he should sacrifice Iphigeneia.*[6] These are Latin themes, but the Greek ones are not much better: *Xenophon refuses to survive Socrates; Solon demands that his laws be rescinded; Demosthenes swears that he did not take the bribe.* The most unrealistic of all subjects, Greek or Latin, however, was: *Cicero deliberates whether he should burn his writings.* As for the *controversiae*, the following example may be cited:[7]

> A husband and wife have sworn that neither shall survive the other. The husband goes on a journey, and sends a messenger to his wife with news of his death. The wife leaps from a cliff, but is rescued and restored to health. She is ordered by her father to desert her husband, but refuses. She is disinherited.

This example is taken from Seneca the Elder, but Quintilian and Tacitus knew many others besides those discussed by Seneca. Tacitus dryly remarked that grand old themes like "the king killer," "the incestuous mother," or "the outraged maid's alternatives" posed situations that rarely came under consideration in the courts. Fronto once sent his student, Marcus Aurelius, the following theme:[8]

> A consul of the Roman people, laying aside his robes, has donned a coat of mail and among the young men at the feast of Minerva has slain a lion in the sight of the Roman people. He is denounced before the Censors.

In some cases we possess not only the proposal of a subject for declamation as in the case of the one above sent by Fronto to Marcus, but we also have the *sermo*, or directions given by the teacher for developing the theme. There was, for example, the *controversia* which had to do with a rich man and a poor youth. The former had financed the latter's education in oratory. Then the rich man was accused of treason and unsuccessfully defended by the youth whom he had befriended. The rich man sued the poor man for ingratitude, a criminal offence. How should the latter defend himself? This, in part, is the *sermo:*[9]

> You understand that this young man must show the greatest respect for his rich patron: that is the way to make it plain that he is acting under necessity.... Those who are greedy of novel situations will easily be tempted here to make the poor man suggest that the rich man is acting in collusion with himself. But were the jury to believe this, they would either sentence him for ... collusion or else for his ingratitude .... Therefore, as far as my judgment goes, the case is one in which the poor man is unwilling to appear; what he says, he says under stress of circumstances.

The Greek practice seems to have differed very little from the Roman. We have a declamation of Lucian's, *The Disinherited,* which is enough to show that even grown men played with these toys. The theme in Lucian's *controversia* had to do with a disinherited son who became a doctor, and after curing his father of seemingly hopeless insanity, was reinstated in his rights. When the youth diagnosed the case of his insane step-mother as incurable, however, he was once more disinherited. In the declamation, Lucian gives the plea of the son for restitution.

Even by the first century A.D. the declamations had become standardized to the extent that some of the better efforts had been preserved and could be studied and admired by subsequent generations of students. As a result, the declamation declined from its original status as a kind of sonata or concerto into (no pun intended) variations on a theme. The students did indeed give recitals for their families and friends. Talented, or ambitious and brazen, youngsters would perform on a moment's notice. Aulus Gellius[10] relates that once when he was vacationing in Naples, a brash young man insisted on giving an exhibition before a distinguished rhetor named Julianus. This orator-to-be brought along his own claquers for the occasion and so antagonized some of the other guests that one of them found an opportunity to propose an insoluble problem for debate. The general tenor of the subject was that seven judges were to hear a case, and the decision of the majority was to determine the penalty. Two judges voted for exile, two for the payment of a fine, and three for the death penalty. Execution was demanded, but the defendant appealed. When the question was proposed, the young orator snapped at the bait and soon displayed his ignorance and lack of talent in a way that was positively embarrassing for everyone except himself. Later, when asked for his opinion, Julianus punned that the young man was eloquent *sine controversia*.

The study of rhetoric was completed by most youths sometime between the ages of eighteen and twenty. While many terminated their education at this point and some might take further training in oratory or go into some specialized field, this sequence of grammatistic, grammar, and rhetoric was the common denominator in education. The full results of this uniform training, however, can not be evaluated unless this survey of the methods employed is combined with some consideration of the authors ordinarily read in the schools. What people read is probably just as important as what they were taught, and it will be useful to identify with some precision and completeness the standard authors, if such there were. This will be a tiresome business, but it is essential for understanding what is yet to be considered: the nature of the intellectual life of the Pax Romana, and the reasons for its sterility.

Quintilian and others *recommended* the reading of certain authors. For the schools of grammar, Quintilian thought that Homer, Virgil, Menander, and some of the old Latin poets would do very well. Dio agreed that Homer should top any list; as a matter of fact, Homer came first with everyone. At the head of the dramatists, Dio would put the tragedies of Euripides and the comedies of Menander. Quintilian rated Euripides, Aristophanes, and Menander first, with Sophocles and Aeschylus after Euripides in tragedy; Plutarch preferred Menander to Aristophanes. In oratory, Demosthenes led every list, but Quintilian and Longinus put Cicero on the same high level. Among the Greek orators Dio rated Lysias and Hyperides second and third; Quintilian's choice was Aeschines and then Hyperides. Plato and Xenophon stood at the head of the philosophers especially with regard to literary excellence; Quintilian agreed with this but would add Cicero. Among the historians, the order was generally Thucydides, first, with Herodotus, second, and both Quintilian and Dio recommended Theopompus. Moreover, Quintilian would confidently match Sallust against Thucydides, or Livy against Herodotus. The importance of the study of poetry was never in doubt. Tacitus rated the Latin poets, Horace, Virgil, and Lucan highly; Quintilian said that Horace was the greatest lyric poet who had written in Latin; he also felt that Lucretius was worth reading, and that Apollonius of Rhodes was important.

The sampling of opinion given above is fairly representative. It might be greatly expanded, but it would give no positive indication of authors commonly read. In his careful study of Lucian, F. W

Householder concerned himself with this problem.[11] He analyzed not only the quotations from, and allusions to, other authors made by Lucian himself, but also compiled similar statistics by combining his analyses of Lucian with the evidence of thirteen other authors of the imperial period. The resultant tabulation gave a list of 56 authors and accounted for over 80% of all the quotations or allusions in the fourteen writers chosen: 23% of the perhaps 12,000 quotations or allusions were from or to Homer, whose nearest competitor was Plato with just over 6%; fourteen authors accounted for over 50% of all quotations and allusions. Householder then compared this material with lists of authors recommended, or assumed to have been used, for study in the schools of grammar and rhetoric. His conclusions are summarized in Table I.

Table I

SCHOOL AUTHORS

A. School of Grammar

Aesop
Homer
Hesiod
Pindar
Euripides
Menander
Thucydides
Herodotus
Demosthenes
Plato

B. School of Rhetoric

The grammar school authors listed in column A, along with:
Stesichorus
Simonides
Alcaeus
Callimachus
Archilochus
Sophocles
Aeschylus
Aristophanes
Lysias
Aeschines
Hyperides
Xenophon
Aristotle
Aeschines Socraticus
Cratinus
Isocrates
Eupolis
Theopompus
Philistus

Table II

Householder's list of quotations and allusions from fourteen authors in order of frequency

1. Homer	29-31. Timaeus
2. Plato	Heraclitus
3. Euripides	Epicharmus
4. Herodotus	32-39. Callimachus
5/6. Hesiod	Alcaeus
Demosthenes	Hyperides
7. Thucydides	Antisthenes
8. Xenophon	Sophron, Philistus
9-11. Sophocles	Gorgias
Aristophanes	Ctesias
Aristotle	40-47. Theognis
12. Aeschylus	Plato Comicus
13. Pindar	Epicurus
14. Menander	Ion, Alexis Comicus
15/16. Archilochus	Aeschines Socraticus
Theophrastus	Hipponax
17. Theopompus	Hippocrates
18/19. Sappho	48-52. Theocritus
Eupolis	Ephorus
20-22. Aesop	Alcman
Chrysippus	Hermippus
Isocrates	Phrynicus Comicus
23-26. Simonides	53-56. Aristoxenus, Hellanicus
Anacreon	Philochorus
Cratinus	Theopompus Comicus
Aeschines	Empedocles
27/28. Stesichorus	
Lysias	

It was significant that 24 of these 29 authors listed in Table I appeared among the first 28 in the list of authors most frequently mentioned by Householder's fourteen selected writers of imperial date; all were in the first 40 (see Table II). Absent from his school list were Theophrastus, Sappho, Chrysippus, and Anacreon; these were numbers 16, 18, 22, and 24 of his first 28. It is worth noting that the last three authors appear in the *scholia* on Dionysius Thrax, and both Theophras-

Table III

Quotations and allusions in eighteen authors of the Pax Romana in order of frequency

	Homer		Epicharmus
	Plato		Aratus
	Euripides		Lysias
	Hesiod		Callimachus
	Xenophon		Hyperides
	Sophocles		Aesop
	Aristophanes		Stesichorus
	Demosthenes		Alcaeus
	Aristotle		Simonides
10)	Pindar	30)	Chrysippus
	Herodotus		Cratinus
	Thucydides		Theognis
	Aeschines		Lycurgus
	Aeschylus		Hippocrates
	Menander		Bacchylides
	Theopompus		
	Archilochus		
	Theophrastus		
	Isocrates		
20)	Sappho		

(Based on Marcus Aurelius, Demetrius of Tarsus, Dio, Lucian, Longinus, Plutarch, Statius, Quintilian, Tacitus, Pliny the Younger, Suetonius, Fronto, Galen, Aulus Gellius, Sextus Empiricus, Persius, Scholia on Dionysius Thrax. The first six also used by Householder).

tus and Chrysippus were read by or at least known to anyone who even dabbled in philosophy.

As a test of Householder's hypothesis, his lists may be checked against others made independently of his study.[12] A list of quotations and allusions in eighteen authors of the Pax Romana, including Greek and Latin writers,[13] yields the order of frequency shown in Table III. We shall discuss the order of this new list presently, but it will be sufficient to note here that the only additions to Householder's lists are Aratus, Theognis, Lycurgus, and Bacchylides; the first two are high on his frequency list for Lucian, and the fourth also appears on the same

list. It is difficult to understand how Householder happened to miss
Lycurgus who is mentioned frequently by Plutarch, Dio, and Lucian
himself; it must have been an oversight. The new list, when compared
with Householder's, lacks Eupolis, Philistus, and Aeschines Socraticus.
It also yields the names of Latin authors. In order of frequency, these
would be:

> Cicero
> Virgil
> Horace
> Pacuvius
> Sallust
> Accius
> Caecilius
> Cato
> Lucretius
> Livy
> Ennius
> Catullus
> Pliny the Elder
> Varro
> Lucilius
> Terence
> Ovid
> Plautus
> Lucan
> Caesar
> Persius
> Suetonius

Pliny the Elder, Varro, and Suetonius were not read in the schools,
but all the others were school authors at one time or another. Cicero,
Virgil, and Caesar were writers with whom even the Greeks admitted
familiarity; Cicero, Virgil, and Sallust are quite well represented in
papyri from Egypt.[14]

Mention of the papyri suggests another approach to the problem of
the school authors. ABout 2500 Greek and Latin literary papyri have
been identified and published. These literary papyri are obviously
important for purely literary studies. Some papyri give us texts of new
authors whose works did not survive through the manuscript tradition.
One might cite the *Hellenica Oxyrhynchia,* a very good history by an
unidentified author, or the novel *Chaireas and Callirrhoe* by Chariton,

and large numbers of poetry fragments. In addition, new works of known authors have come to light in the papyri: hitherto unknown plays by the Athenian dramatists of the fifth century, our only texts of Menander's comedies, and many lost poems of Sappho, Alcaeus, Bacchylides, and others. A very important discovery was the papyrus text of the *Constitution of Athens,* attributed to Aristotle, which was found about 1890. Even new fragments of Latin authors have turned up; particularly noteworthy are parts of Livy and Sallust. The literary papyri are also valuable from another point of view: it is possible to employ them in the reconstruction of social, intellectual, and literary history. Their evidence can be used to supplement that of the manuscript tradition in several ways.

The manuscript tradition was formed by a selective process. Manuscripts were copied and recopied through the ages after the end of antiquity. This perpetuation was largely the work of churchmen in Eastern and Western Christendom. Naturally, the special interests and prejudices of the Christians were influential in determining what was rejected or chosen for perpetuation. Plato, Cicero, and Virgil, for example, were authors particularly congenial to the men of the Middle Ages, while Lucretius was not acceptable. Even before the end of the classical period, various fads and fancies were at work. The Alexandrian Canon, which selected the ten "best" orators, the three "best" writers of tragedy, etc., encouraged the perpetuation of some texts and the neglect of others. Again, because of the difficulty and expense of copying manuscripts, larger works tended to be replaced by condensations and epitomes; thus, for example, much of Livy was lost. Moreover, there was a curious feeling that if several authors dealt with the same subject, only the best or the preferred treatment was worth keeping. Gresham's law was given a reverse twist, and the "best" drove the "worst" out of circulation.

The manuscript tradition, therefore, leaves us with an "end product" which has certain disadvantages when compared with the literary papyri, for the papyri allow us to observe at first hand the tastes and preferences of certain periods *in antiquity.* While it must be admitted that the papyri probably reflect the tastes of a particular area of the ancient world (Egypt), it is nevertheless possible to ask of the papyri such questions as: What were the "classics" of the second century A.D.? What were the contemporary interests in authors, styles, and subjects? The papyri also provide information about the educational procedures in the Egyptian schools and the part played by literature in this education.

Although the earliest literary papyri date from the third century

B.C. and the latest from the seventh or eighth centuries A.D., the majority come from the first three centuries of the Christian era. It is significant that Homeric papyri number over 500. The closest rivals of Homer are Euripides (about 100), Demosthenes (about 75), Callimachus (about 70), and finally Hesiod with about 60. Other authors represented by texts numbering between 20-45 are Aeschylus, Plato, Aristophanes, Isocrates, Thucydides, Xenophon, Menander, Herodotus, Pindar, Sappho, and Virgil. The Latin authors represented are Cicero, Juvenal, Livy, Lucan, Sallust, and Terence (in addition to Virgil).

An analysis of papyri from the second century A.D. confirms the evidence of the manuscript tradition that there was a basic literature which included most of the distinguished authors of earlier times. The tables of comparison included below reveal an amazing uniformity in the ranking of authors. These tables or lists are based on allusions and quotations and on the relative numbers of the papyri found for each author. It will be clear that certain authors were read and known to educated people everywhere, but there was also a Greek world and a Latin world of literature even though some authors were common property. It is worth noting, too, that the Greek world of literature as represented by Dio, Plutarch, and Lucian corresponds very nearly with the literary cosmos of Egypt as revealed in the papyri. The main difference is to be seen in the popularity in Egypt of the "national" poets, Callimachus and Apollonius. Table IV (opposite) will be self-explanatory.

In 1923 C. H. Oldfather[15] in his study of the literary papyri attempted to draw up a list of authors represented in the school texts of the second century A.D. One of his criteria for distinguishing a school text from a non-school text was whether the *verso* (back side) of the papyrus had been used to receive the particular text in question. That is, in many cases a non-school text (an account, a letter, etc.) would appear on the *recto,* and then later the *verso* would have been used as scratch paper in the schools. The appearance of different hands on the *recto* and *verso* would lend credence to this hypothesis. Oldfather's list included Archilochus, Callimachus, Euripides, Hesiod, Homer, Hyperides, Isocrates, Menander, Pindar, Sophocles, Thucydides, Apollonius of Rhodes, and Hippocrates. All but the last two are shown by Householder's list to have been school authors, but the rating of Apollonius on the papyrus list (Table IV) and also on the Latin list suggests that he was a school author in Egypt and the West; moreover, the appearance of Hippocrates in Table III (p. 39) seems to be a point in favor of including him among the school authors. In some cases where the identification of the papyri as school texts was doubtful

Table IV

	I	H	Papyri	Gram. Gr.	Latin
Homer	1G	1	1	1	1
Plato	2G	2	6	10	2
Euripides	3G	3	2	3	3
Hesiod	4G	5	5	5	4
Xenophon	5R	8	11		6
Sophocles	6R	9	14		9
Aristophanes	7R	10	7	2	10
Demosthenes	8G	6	3	7	5
Aristotle	9R	11	16	9	19
Pindar	10G	13	15	12	11
Herodotus	11G	4	10	8	13
Thucydides	12G	7	8	11	12
Aeschines	13R	26			8
Aeschylus	14R	12	13		20
Menander	15G	14	12	6	7
Theopompus	16R	17			14
Archilochus	17R	15			21
Theophrastus	18	16			15
Isocrates	19R	22	9		22
Sappho	20	18	17	13	23
Epicharmus	21	31			
Aratus	22				
Lysias	23R	28			
Callimachus	24R	32	4	4	17
Hyperides	25R	34			
Aesop	26G	20			16
Stesichorus	27R				
Alcaeus	28	33			
Simonides	29R	23			
Chrysippus	30	21			
Cratinus	31R	25			
Theognis	32	40			
Lycurgus	33				
Hippocrates	34	47			
Bacchylides	35				
Apollonius of Rhodes			18		18

Legend:
I   Eighteen authors of Pax Romana (Table III)
G   Grammar School author
R   Author read in school of rhetoric
H   Householder (fourteen authors — Table II)
Papyri   Number of papyri in order of frequency
Gram. Gr.   Frequency in Grammatici Graeci
Latin   Latin authors separated from Greek authors of Table III

Table V

Revised List of School Authors

A. School of Grammar

Aesop	Demosthenes
Homer	Plato
Hesiod	Pindar
Euripides	Sappho ?
Menander	Alcaeus ?
Thucydides	Epicharmus ?
Herodotus	Hippocrates ?

B. School of Rhetoric
(authors listed under A as well as B)

Sophocles	Isocrates	Theophrastus
Aeschylus	Lysias	Aristotle
Aristophanes	Aeschines	Aeschines
Cratinus	Hyperides	Socraticus
Eupolis	Lycurgus	Theophrastus

Archilochus	Apollonius
Alcman	Callimachus
Theognis	Aratus
Anacreon	
Bacchylides	
Stesichorus	
Simonides	

Theopompus
Philistus

N.B. Question marks indicate uncertainty whether authors were part of curriculum of grammar or rhetoric

Oldfather was inclined to think that Aristophanes, Demosthenes, and Xenophon were studied in the schools; this guess is confirmed by Householder's list. To the original 29 authors identified by Householder, then, several may be added: Sappho, Anacreon, Apollonius, Hippocrates, and very probably Aratus, Theognis, Bacchylides, Alcman, Epicharmus, and Lycurgus. The further addition of Theophrastus, who seems a very likely possibility, would give a nice round 40 for a total and leave Chrysippus as the only outsider.

The lists of authors (Table IV) most frequently quoted or alluded to are instructive, to say the least. With the exception of Chrysippus, they appear to contain the names of school authors whose works every educated person had read by the time he was eighteen years of age. How much reading did the average educated person do after that time? It is disturbing that the Greek list includes no author later than the third century B.C.; and, worse still, of the fifteen authors most frequently employed for illustration or authority, nine were read in the schools of grammar; the top five on the Latin list of Greek authors are all in this category. We shall have occasion to refer again to the overwhelming predominance of Homer, for this is a matter of great importance. The literary excellence of most of these authors is, of course, beyond question, but the list shows the standardization and rather circumscribed nature of the curriculum of the Pax Romana.

⊕

After the completion of the rhetorical training, the formal education of many persons came to an end. There were some who continued their study of oratory, and there were others who went on to study law, medicine, or philosophy. Outside these fields, advanced instruction might be had with some specialist in mathematics or astronomy. Those who did not become doctors, lawyers, or scientists often felt that there was a hierarchy of studies which began with grammatistic, grammar, and rhetoric, and then went on to oratory and finally to philosophy. The philosophers were loud in their claims to superiority, although the higher ranking of philosophy was not accepted by all the orators. Dio went from oratory to philosophy and was very proud of himself. Lucian, on the other hand, held a low opinion of philosophers. Fronto was very unhappy when his prize pupil, Marcus Aurelius, defected to philosophy. In no less than three letters he poured out his objections; twice he made the point that philosophy took much less study, training, and ability than oratory. In another letter to a friend he expressed his views very succinctly: "Cornelianus is a good man and a friend of mine and no philosopher."

Quintilian also remarked that some people who found the study of oratory too difficult became lawyers, while others turned to philosophy. He sneered that a man could make a pretence of philosophy but not of eloquence.[16] Galen, on the other hand, was convinced in his own mind that he had managed to double in brass by becoming both a physician and a philosopher; at one point, he wrote an essay to prove that the best physician must also be a philosopher.

With these rival claims in mind, we may follow the youth of the Pax Romana into manhood in order to see how their education was employed as they took up divers avocations and professions and began to face the business of living.

FOOTNOTES

1. Among the best are: H–I. Marrou, *History of Education in Antiquity*, London 1956; A. Gwynn, *Roman Education*, Oxford 1926; A. S. Wilkins, *Roman Education*, Cambridge 1905; Appendix III in F. W. Householder, *Literary Quotation and Allusion in Lucian*, New York 1941.

2. Sextus Empiricus, *Against the Professors*, I, 4 ff.

3. For examples, see Marrou, *op. cit.*, Part III, Chapter IV.

4. H. Nettleship, "The Study of Latin Grammar among the Romans in the First Century A.D.," *Lectures and Essays*, Second Series, Oxford 1895, pp. 144-171.

5. On this and what follows, see the excellent summary of Householder, *op. cit.*, p. 80 ff.

6. W. A. Edmond, *The Suasoriae of Seneca the Elder*, Cambridge 1928; S. F. Bonner, *Roman Declamation*, Liverpool 1949.

7. Extract taken from A. Gwynn, *Roman Education*, Oxford 1926, p. 160 by permission of the Clarendon Press, Oxford.

8. Reprinted by permission of the publishers from C. R. Haines, *Marcus Aurelius Fronto*, Cambridge, Mass.: Harvard University Press, 1919. The passage is from Vol. I, p. 211.

9. Extract taken from A. Gwynn, *Roman Education*, p. 214, by permission of the Clarendon Press, Oxford.

10. Aulus Gellius, *Attic Nights*, IX, 15.

11. See Householder, *op. cit.*, pp. 44, 45, 56, 63.

12. The lists are my own, compiled several years before reading Householder's dissertation.

13. Householder used Marcus Aurelius, Demetrius, Dio, Lucian, Longinus, Plutarch, Aelian, Scholia on Aristophanes, Athenaeus, Dionysius of Halicarnassus, Maximus, Pausanias, Julius Pollux, and the Rhetores Graeco. For my list, see Table III.

14. R. Pack, *The Greek and Roman Literary Texts from Greco-Roman Egypt*, Ann Arbor 1952, p. 95 ff.

15. *The Greek Literary Texts from Greco-Roman Egypt* (in University of Wisconsin *Studies in the Social Sciences*, no. 9), Madison 1923.

16. Quintilian, *Institutes*, XII, 3, 12.

Pedants and Critics

It is a difficult task to give novelty to what is old, authority to what is new, brilliance to the to the commonplace, light to the obscure, attraction to the stale....

Pliny the Elder

Much learning does not make a scholar.

Aulus Gellius

A FAIR AMOUNT of scholarly ditchdigging went forward in the first two centuries of the Christian era. Most of the effort was expended in the area of language and literature. On the Latin side, to mention a few examples, Palaemon and the elder Pliny wrote on grammar; Valerius Probus provided reliable texts of Virgil, Horace, Lucretius, and Persius; Festus abridged the lexicon of Verrius Flaccus. Across the way, the dyscolic Apollonius is reputed to have put Greek grammar on a scientific footing, while his son, Herodian, worked on accentuation, and Hephaestion dealt with metre. Greek lexicography flourished with the revival of Atticism in oratory: Pamphilus, Aelius Dionysius, Harpocration, Pollux, and Phrynichus labored to fill the arsenal of the orators. The new sophists resembled our birdmen of today: it took an army of grammarians, rhetoricians, and lexicographers on the ground to keep one of them in the air. The popularity of rhetoric led naturally to the writing of handbooks and textbooks: the works of Alexander, Theon, Demetrius of Tarsus, Hermogenes, Quintilian, and the elder Seneca are representative of this activity.

Most of these laborers were teachers. By profession and by natural inclination they were destined to grub, but there were also amateurs who had acquired some kind of academic fixation in the course of their schooling and kept up their homework for the rest of their lives. Pliny the Elder, Aulus Gellius, and Galen are the names that come to mind when avocational scholarship is mentioned, but there were others who busied themselves in a similar manner.

While the industry of the teachers is hard to assess, that of the amateurs seems to have been boundless. Quintilian complained that people wasted time in sociability, sleep, and ceremony instead of devoting themselves to study, but he could not have criticised the elder Pliny who made every moment count. Pliny's "incredible zeal and wakefulness beyond compare" are described in a famous letter by his nephew.[1] At meals, during his sunbath, on the road, Pliny was constantly being read to, taking notes, or dictating. He maintained that no matter how bad a book might be, something of value could be gleaned from it. As his *Natural History* shows, his charity far exceeded his judgement. Aulus Gellius, too, burned the midnight oil "unrolling and running through many a scroll"; his perspicacity, probably less than Pliny's to start with, sagged under the weight of many volumes. Galen was another tireless worker, but his non-medical research, he felt, paid good dividends:

> People who are unused to learning, learn little, and that slowly, while those more accustomed do much more and do it more easily. The same thing also happens with research. Those who are altogether unfamiliar with this become blinded and bewildered as soon as their minds begin to work: they readily withdraw from the inquiry, in a state of mental fatigue and exhaustion, much like people who attempt to race without having been trained. He, on the other hand, who is accustomed to research, seeks and penetrates everywhere mentally, passing constantly from one topic to another; nor does he ever give up his investigation; he pursues it not merely for a matter of days, but throughout his whole life. Also by transferring his mind to other ideas which are not yet foreign to the question at issue, he persists till he reaches the solution.[2]

Much of the "research" of Pliny, Aulus Gellius, Marcus Aurelius, and even Galen consisted merely of reading and taking notes or abstracting. Galen[3] confessed that he prepared notes for his forgetful old age and to oblige his friends. Aulus Gellius made excerpts and notes as he went along and never tried to put them in any logical order. The elder Pliny left his nephew 160 volumes of notes "written in a very small character"; for his *Natural History* alone he read 2,000 volumes. Although Pliny organized his effort a little better than did Aulus Gellius, both had the consideration to provide a table of contents. Not everyone followed this method, however, and not everyone was as discriminating as Gellius. He himself is our authority for this:

> A friend of mine.... presenting me with a book of great bulk, as he himself put it, with learning of every kind.... said that he had

compiled it as the result of wide, varied, and abstruse reading.... I took the book eagerly....and shut myself up in order to read it without interruption. But what was written there was.... merely a list of curiosities: the name of the man who was first called a grammarian.... the names of the companions of Ulysses who were seized and torn to pieces by Scylla.... a list of the isopsephic verses in Homer....[4]

Just as the works on Greek and Latin grammar, lexicography, and rhetoric mirrored the consuming interests of the age and pretty well outnumbered other scholarly productions, so also nearly half of the 388 sections or chapters in the twenty volumes of the *Attic Nights* were devoted to lexicography, grammar, etymology, and style. This, however, is not the whole story, since a further analysis of the items included by Aulus Gellius suggests that his "scholarly" interests and very probably those of his contemporaries were on the level of the elementary or grammar school rather than that of the rhetorical establishment. It will be recalled that grammar was divided into three parts: historical, technical, and special. No less than 264 of the chapters in Aulus Gellius are on the level of the school of grammar: there are 114 items to be classed as historical, mostly little anecdotes of the kind to be found in the work of Valerius Maximus which was the principal school manual in this department; in the special category may be listed 66 items on lexicography; and under technical come 38 on grammar, 26 on etymology, and 20 on textual criticism and translation. Of the remainder, 21 chapters on literary history or criticism might be on the rhetorical level, 10 are miscellaneous or non-academic, 26 deal with medicine and science (charitably speaking), 26 with legal and constitutional matters, and 41 with philosophy including ethics, dialectic, and snippets about the various systems; these philosophical gleanings were from Aulus Gellius' student days in Athens.

When all is said and done, it is the handbooks and textbooks of this age that are most impressive. Admittedly lacking in originality and primarily based upon older and possibly better works now lost, they nevertheless have virtues of clarity and organization that are entirely lacking from the products of "research." People have not had much trouble in finding things to criticize about Quintilian's *Institutes,* but it is a good, and very nearly a great, work. The treatise *On Style,* probably written by a friend of Plutarch named Demetrius of Tarsus, is not in the same high class with the *Institutes,* but it is clear and well organized and was doubtless never intended to fulfill any higher purpose than to provide a set of lecture notes.

The basic subject treated by Demetrius was the art of prose writing. Although his interest was more in expression than thought, Demetrius has been praised for the soundness of his precepts and the fundamentally permanent value of his book.[5] He divided his treatise into five parts: the first (Book I) was taken up with preliminary remarks and definitions, and the remaining four described the virtues and pitfalls of what he called the elevated, elegant, plain, and forcible styles. By way of illustration, passages were quoted from the ancient authors; Homer, Plato, Demosthenes, Xenophon, Thucydides, and Sappho were the writers most frequently drawn upon for examples.

The elevated style, which derives from a certain kind of composition, subject matter, and diction, is said by Demetrius to be well represented in Thucydides and Plato. In Thucydides he finds impressive prose rhythms dignified by the judicious use of long syllables; there is also a wonderful marshalling of words for effect. Thucydides, says Demetrius, has the air of a man stumbling on a rough road, but there is often a use of rugged words in a rugged arrangement that is impressive. Demetrius quotes the famous "from other maladies this year, by common consent, was free," and shows that an alternative, more normal word order, "by common consent this year was free from other maladies," would be much less effective. Plato, too, could marshall his words for vivid effects and heightened these by making each succeeding phrase more vivid than the last. The example quoted is: "when a man suffers music to play upon him and to flood his soul through his ears." The versatile Homer, a poet of many styles, is called upon for an illustration of augmented hyperbole in his description of the Cyclops:.... not like to the sons of men, but seeming a forest-clad summit." Concurrence of vowels, that will "make the verses clang," is to be avoided; on this point Roberts, the editor and translator of Demetrius, very cleverly quotes Pope's "though oft the ear the open vowels tire." On the other hand, says Demetrius, words can be made to chime if not run together; instead of καλά ὅτιν it is possible to write πάντα μὲν τὰ νέα κἀὶ καλά ἐστιν.

Elevation, however, was not merely a matter of composition; it could only be successful when dealing with great subjects, and the diction must also be superior, distinguished, and inclined to the unfamiliar. This might often be accomplished by the use of metaphor, a thing in which Plato was very skillful or, if a metaphor seemed too daring, it might be converted into a simile; Xenophon, for example, was inclined to use similes rather than metaphors. It was comforting and reassuring to know that "usage is our teacher everywhere," and it has clothed almost all concepts in metaphors. Compound words, onomatopoeic words, and allegory might be used impressively also. The danger of the elevated style was that it might lapse into frigidity when one overshot the mark with extravagant and impossible thought, inappropriate diction, or a lack of good rhythm. The style must always suit the subject, Demetrius warns again, and one must be especially careful about hyperbole. Sappho was extremely daring in her use of hyperbole but always managed to get away with it. Hyperbole transcends the possible; that is why it is so effective in comedy and so dangerous to use elsewhere.

The elegant style, as exemplified by Plato, Herodotus, and Xenophon, is discussed in Book III by Demetrius under much the same general headings; the plain style, useful for narration, persuasion, and letter-writing (sometimes a combination of the elegant and the plain) comes in Book IV; and the work ends with a discussion of the forcible style with Demosthenes as its principal exponent. Affectation, aridity, and the unpleasant, the undesirable corollaries of these three styles, are also included and analyzed.

Demetrius, clearly a Peripatetic indebted to Aristotle and Theophrastus, was not distinguished by the novelty of his thought or a radical approach to his subject. A century earlier Dionysius of Halicarnassus in his work on literary composition had talked about the "beautiful" style of Thucydides with its grandeur and dignity or the "charming" style of Xenophon characterized by freshness and grace. He had distinguished an austere mode of composition employed by Pindar, Aeschylus, and Thucydides; a smooth (or florid) mode exemplified by Euripides and Isocrates; and a harmonious blend of the two found in Homer, Sophocles, Demosthenes, and Plato.[6] Dionysius had shown that the arrangement of words was more important than the words themselves and had made transpositions of words to show that the effects achieved by certain passages were not due to the words or the thought but to the arrangement. Favorinus, the idol of Aulus Gellius, apparently did not share the views of Dionysius on arrangement, for he said that to change a single word in Plato and substitute another word for it would mar the elegance of style, while to do the same with Lysias would obscure the meaning.[7]

For Dionysius the key words were sound, variety, rhythm, and appropriateness. He discovered, to his own satisfaction if not to that of others, the existence of two styles in Plato: one was a good, plain style, simple and precise, while the other was ornate and something of a failure; he blamed the faults of this second style on the influence of Gorgias. Dionysius also found the influence of Gorgias at work in Thucydides where there was strange diction and an unorthodox construction that turned phrases into words, words into phrases, inverted the ordinary uses of nouns and verbs, and interchanged active and passive verbs. One of the most penetrating remarks of Dionysius was that the rules contained in the rhetorical manuals would not suffice as a complete guide to good composition; most rules might be safely disregarded or violated.[8]

All of this leads us into the difficult and perplexing matter of criticism in antiquity. The "new critics" and the ancient critics have very little in common as far as one can tell at the moment, and thus the ancients seem very antiquated indeed. Of course, a large part of ancient criticism has undoubtedly been lost; most of what we have for the period of the Pax Romana is concerned with oratory.

By the second century A.D. there was a tendency to disregard the relative and to adopt an absolute standard: the "doctrine of classicism" had won the field. The modernists of the first century had been routed, and, it has been said that "men turned with a sure instinct to the works of classical Greece, accepting them, and them only, as the models for literature, and drawing from them principles to guide their own efforts."[9] This statement is essentially true, but it requires some qualification and elaboration. A survey of criticism in the first and second centuries A.D. will suggest its limitations and may also help to explain why criticism tended to take certain forms and attitudes.

Much of the criticism from the period of the Pax Romana occurs in the manuals where it is introduced for the purpose of practical instruction, but the age also produced authors who wrote criticism for its own sake. There is Greek literary criticism, and there is Latin literary criticism. The second depended on the first in several ways, yet the Latin criticism did, in certain ways, stand by itself. The Greek critics dealt almost exclusively with Greek literature; the Latin critics were concerned with their own literature but did not neglect the Greek although their ideas about it were more often borrowed than original. An earlier example of precisely this tendency may be found in Horace who had nothing new to say about Greek literature but was quite independent when he dealt with the Latin.[10]

There was variety and considerable difference of level in the criticism which dealt with Latin authors. It ranged all the way from the literary biographies written by Suetonius to the rather sophisticated *Dialogus* of Tacitus and the strictures of the poets on their own art and its practitioners. Aulus Gellius rates more than a sentence in the history of Latin literary criticism, not so much for his own personal contribution to it, though he does have some ideas of his own, but more because he records the opinions of Valerius Probus, Favorinus,

Julianus, and others. People were still concerned with establishing the authorship of the one hundred and thirty plays attributed to Plautus. Lists had been made by Varro, Aelius, Sedigitus, and others, but there was little agreement among them; some would assign twenty-five plays, and others as many as one hundred and twenty, to Plautus. The surest test lay in the style and diction, said Aulus Gellius, and he demonstrated the use of this method of identification. "Virgil Studies" were in a popular stage in the second century. People traced the borrowings of Virgil from Homer, Parthenius, Lucretius, Hesiod, Theocritus, and Apollonius, and they evaluated his success, or lack of it, in imitating or adapting these authors.[11] Aulus Gellius has a very interesting evaluation of the treatment of the same theme by Pindar and Virgil. Julianus, the old teacher of Aulus, once discussed the imitation of Ennius by Virgil; although Julianus explained clearly and impressively his point of view, there was some disillusionment in store because "afterwards I ran across the very same remarks in some very well-known handbooks." Gellius himself became interested in a comedy by Menander that had been translated by Caecilius. He had always felt that the Latin play was very good until he read the Greek original which was infinitely more brilliant; by comparing the two versions he could see how, time after time, Caecilius had simply failed to catch the excellence of Menander. Ennius' adaptation of Euripides, the style of Sallust and his possible use of poetic circumlocution, and the merits of Cicero are also discussed in chapters of the *Attic Nights*.

By the second century, the younger Seneca, one of the "modernists" who had enjoyed a great vogue in his own lifetime, was the subject of much adverse criticism. Gellius himself, although he noted this hostility, refused to pass judgment on Seneca as a writer; he felt that Seneca had little merit as a critic and took particular exception to Seneca's disparagement of Ennius, Cicero, and Virgil. Fronto, on the other hand, was openly hostile to Seneca: in a letter to Marcus Aurelius he spoke of the "soft and hectic plums of Seneca," who was a juggler fit only to amuse schoolboys; there were some clever expressions, and sometimes a little dignity, but these were few and far between "like finding silver coins in a sewer."[12] Quintilian's judgment of Seneca was a little more kind; he felt he could safely entrust Seneca to a mature reader who would not be carried away by the spectacular elements in his style but would be able to see both the good and bad points of it. Quintilian could not condone, however, the attacks of Seneca on authors who were certainly his superiors.[13]

This was a difficult time for the critic of Latin literature, for his judgements were unavoidably influenced by what had happened and what was happening on the Greek side. Historically, Latin literature had developed under the influence of Greek literature; it had passed from mere translation and crude imitation of Greek models in the third century B.C. to a maturity in the Ciceronian and Augustan periods in which Cicero, Catullus, Sallust, Horace, and Virgil had exploited to the fullest the possibilities of a literature and a language which had had to develop in constricting proximity to another language and literature that was not only already fully matured but invested with an overwhelming prestige. Where could Latin literature go after the Augustan Age? Latin authors were forced to experiment with new things, but at the same time they could not help being influenced by the contemporary Greek trends toward classicism. The "modernists" of the first century therefore had not only to discover something that would meet with general acceptance, but also they had to combat a regressive trend in Latin which followed the backtracking movement in Greek literature. In the second century B.C., almost before they had a literature, the Romans had begun to think in terms of literary canons — to make lists of the best Latin poets, orators, and the like — merely because this canonization had already taken place on the Greek side.[14] When the new Atticism began to triumph in Greek literature, the Romans were stimulated to define what was "classic" in Latin. The decision was not a difficult one to make, for Cicero, Virgil, and their contemporaries stood head and shoulders above those who had either preceded or followed them.

The victory of Latin classicism was inevitable but not easily won. The "modernists" died hard. In addition, many who rejected the modernism of Seneca and his school were not willing wholly to accept classicism. Some, like Fronto, experimented with archaism. Moreover, there were sensible people who realized that, while classicism might correct the abuses of the experimenters, the acceptance of an absolute standard might promote sterility.

In the *Dialogus* of Tacitus one finds the clearest expression of the literary perplexity which prevailed at the close of the first century. The *Dialogus* has been praised as far and away the finest extant work of Latin literary criticism.[15] A master stroke was the choice of the dialogue form because it allowed the expression of several points of view and thus avoided the dogmatism of most ancient criticism; it made possible an inquiry rather than the usual statement of rules. Three questions were considered, and, as in the typical Socratic dialogue, no firm conclusion was reached. On the other hand, the arguments pro and con were presented in an unsocratic manner; that is, all the participants had a fighting chance instead of being sparring mates for a protagonist.

After a discussion of the relative merits of oratory and poetry, there was a full review of the arguments for and against the acceptance of the Ciceronian style as classic and as the model for present and future orators. Finally, there was an inquiry into the causes of the decline of oratory. These were said to be ethical or educational or the result of an age that provided neither the occasion nor the stimulus for great oratory. The inconclusive nature of this discussion has sometimes been criticized; it has been said that Tacitus looks one way and rows another.[16] Other critics have felt that Tacitus, while adopting the Ciceronian standard, was nevertheless concerned with the perils of adherence to an absolute which might or might not provide a suitable form for every age; it might be better for each generation to work out its own salvation.[17]

Some heretic may some day argue that the *Dialogus* is no more than a successful rhetorical exercise. Cicero had used the dialogue form with reasonable success; there are certain obvious parallels between his *Brutus,* which employed the dialogue form, and the *Dialogus* of Tacitus. Furthermore, the *Dialogus* was by no means unique in its arguments and theories. Quintilian had blamed the decline of oratory on the failure of education, and Longinus had selected moral decay as his chief cause at the same time rejecting the argument that the fall of the republic was chiefly responsible for the sad state into which oratory had fallen. Longinus, in fact, treated this subject in such a way as to suggest that it was a common topic of discussion. Although he was definitely in the Ciceronian camp, Quintilian was very specific in his injunctions against simple imitation and insistent that each age must strive to improve and discover new things. The attitude that poetry is inferior to oratory is expressed by one of the participants in Tacitus' dialogue who says that unsuccessful lawyers take up the writing of poetry,[18] while in the *Satyricon*[19] it is said that poetry is the hobby of retired advocates.

As a critic, Quintilian was definitely inferior to Tacitus. He said nothing original about Greek literature, and most of his remarks about the Latin writers seemed to lack penetration. Nettleship's verdict was that Quintilian's criticisms on the Latin side were vitiated by the idea of making canons of the Latin authors to correspond as closely as possible with the Greek canons; Quintilian's comments were brief and hurried, and it was only in speaking of Cicero that he generated any enthusiasm.[20]

Petronius in the *Satyricon* had a number of things to say about intellectual and artistic decline: rhetoricians had ruined oratory with the help of parents who would not insist on high standards; avarice and greed had damaged the liberal arts; philosophy, astronomy, sculpture, and science had suffered along with oratory. "We can only criticize antiquity and devote all our energies, in precept and practice, to the faults of the old masters." In his criticism of contemporary poetry Petronius, through Eumolpus, satirized Lucan. He also seemed to be hostile to Persius and Seneca.

Here and there, of course, one finds bits of criticism in the poets themselves. False classicism was condemned by Persius, Martial, and Juvenal, all of whom found it more congenial to deal with the contemporary scene in which they found more than enough to criticize and satirize.[21] Persius was bitter about the modern poets who could only pant in the grand style, gargle, and roll their eyes. Their poetry was sissy stuff; one no longer heard virile poetry of the older kind accompanied by "the smack of nails bitten to the quick."

The Greeks of the Pax Romana did not waste much effort in applying literary criticism to their contemporary literature. Instead, they concentrated on the great figures of the past. It is rather curious, and probably significant, that, just as most Latin criticism was concerned with Virgil, so Greek activity centered on Homer. Dio noted the boldness of Homer who mingled many Greek dialects in his poems, introduced barbarian words, used words both old and new and even coined many of his own, employed onomatopoeia, and was a master of metaphor. Dio and Plutarch agreed on the ethical value and wisdom of Homer whose poems were fit even for the education of kings. They also talked about the allegorical interpretation of Homer. His greatness was such that all others must be measured by his standard; thus, Dio compared Homer and Socrates, and Lucian compared and contrasted Homer and Demosthenes.

A quixotic attempt to challenge the supremacy of Homer which occurred in the time of Hadrian may perhaps be interpreted as evidence of a revolt against classicism. Cassius Dio says that Hadrian "abolished Homer and introduced Antimachus in his stead."[22] This was the epic poet, Antimachus of Colophon (*fl.* 400 B.C.), author of the *Thebais* and a poor second to Homer according to Quintilian. It was also said that Hadrian wrote a poem, called *Catachannae,* in the style of Antimachus. This was probably the point of a letter written by Marcus Aurelius to Fronto in which he said:[23]

I saw there a tree with many branches, which he called by its proper name of *catachanna.* But it seemed to me a new and extraordinary tree, bearing as it did upon its single stem off-shoots of almost every kind of tree...

And in a letter to Marcus Aurelius, Fronto spoke of hybrid eloquence of the *catachanna* type which ought to be plucked up by the roots.[24]

The attack on Homer may have been implemented by a revival of the old story that Hesiod had defeated Homer in a contest of poetry at Chalcis. The tale was made the subject of a poem during the reign of Hadrian.[25] Echoes of the controversy may also be seen in a renewal of the dispute over the age of Homer and Hesiod; people argued about whether one had preceded the other or whether they were really contemporaries.[26] It is also interesting to note that a second century papyrus of Antimachus has been found.[27]

One of the methods of criticism, applied as in the case of Homer above, was a comparison of authors. Dionysius of Halicarnassus had long before made a comparison of Herodotus and Thucydides. In the second century Plutarch compared Aristophanes and Menander. Although one of his basic objections was to the coarseness and vulgarity of Aristophanes, Plutarch also argued the superiority of Menander on the basis of style and artistry: Menander was polished, refined, a writer of beautiful poetry who was careful to have his characters speak in a manner appropriate to their nature and station in life; Aristophanes could not match the poetry of Menander nor did he take the pains to be consistent in the portrayal of character or the writing of dialogue. One of the very best efforts of Dio was his comparison of the way in which Aeschylus, Sophocles, and Euripides handled the story of Philoctetes. Not only did Dio do this with insight, but also he managed to get through it with less than a half dozen references to Homer.

An entirely different approach to the drama is found in an unusual treatise which seems to date from the first century A.D. This is the *Tractatus Coislinianus,* an anonymous work which discusses the nature of comedy.[28] A product of Peripatetic thought, the treatise is clearly based on some more extensive original and ultimately upon the now lost second book of Aristotle's *Poetics.* The *Tractatus* is a mere skeleton or outline, but it does contain matters of interest. Poetry is said to be non-mimetic and mimetic. In the first category fall the historical epics like that of Choerilus and didactic *(Works and Days)* or theoretical poetry *(Theogony).* Mimetic poetry includes narrative *(Odyssey)* or dramatic types; under dramatic the sub-categories are comedy, tragedy, mimes, and satyr plays. Comedy is defined as the imitation of an action that is ludicrous or imperfect. Comedy purges the emotions through pleasure and laughter in the same way that tragedy produces catharsis through compassion and terror. Laughter may be evoked by diction or by the content or action of a play. Garrulity, the use of diminutives, puns, unusual grammar and syntax, homonyms, synonyms, and paronyms may be used to cause laughter through diction, while in the action deception, the use of the impossible, the unexpected, the non sequitur, and so on down to clownish dancing may bring a laugh. Metaphor and hyperbole are discussed, the elements of the comic plot are analyzed, and the old, new, and middle comedy are characterized respectively as laughable, serious, and mixed.

There are echoes of some of this in Dionysius of Halicarnassus and Demetrius of Tarsus. The latter had discussed comedy under the heading of the graceful or elegant style, showing the effectiveness of hyperbole, and warning that humor could be spoiled by verbal adornment: "the elaboration of humor is like beautifying an ape."[29] Cicero and Quintilian also dealt with the subject of laughter. Quintilian noted that there was no teacher in this department.[30] Laughter resulted from something said or done; the desire to incite laughter might stem from some gay or inoffensive purpose or from a bitter and malicious mood. Quintilian knew that Tiro had published three volumes of Cicero's jests. Most of the wit that Quintilian retails for the purposes of illustration must have been stale then, and its recent use by the so-called comics of television has done little to freshen it. Nothing, apparently, has more cultural staying power than a bad joke. One example will be more than enough: a lady announces that she is thirty years of age, and the gentleman replies that this is what she has been telling him for the last twenty years! The Roman man in the street and our televiewers clearly have much in common.

Turning from the ridiculous to the *Sublime,* we come naturally to Longinus. His *Peri Hypsous* has been called a golden book; it is considered to mark the apex of Greek literary criticism in the Roman period. Beyond a doubt the enthusiasm of Longinus is contagious. His work makes a great impression on its first reading, but some of the glitter fades after more careful study especially after reading other Greek and Latin critics who deal with sublimity in literature and related arts. Longinus and Demetrius of Tarsus, for example, have much in common, although Longinus is concerned with both thought and expression while Demetrius concentrates on the latter; moreover, Longinus deals only with the elevated style, and Demetrius considers the other three styles as well. There is much in Tacitus and Quintilian, too, that is reminiscent of the treatise of Longinus *On the Sublime.*

The sublime is defined by Longinus as excellence of expression, or true grandeur of expression which is the product of natural ability combined with art (technique). It is said by Longinus that if a thought will not bear repetition, it lacks sublimity. The true test of greatness is not the applause of the moment but the verdict of time.

The natural sources of the sublime are grandeur of thought and passion, but they must be supplemented by certain artificial aids: figures of speech, noble phrasing, and the careful and suitable arrangement of words. Failure to achieve sublimity may result from a number of causes. Some writers overshoot the mark through bombast or tumidity; a striving for what is artificial and high-flown may lead to puerility; others use passion out of place and without meaning where passion is not required; still others, straining after novelty, achieve only frigidity. Timaeus, it is noted, is especially given to frigidity, but even Plato and Xenophon succumb to it at times.

Homer, of course, is the most sublime of all authors. Longinus notes, however, that there is a notable difference between the *Iliad* and the *Odyssey*. It does not occur to him that the poems might be the work of two authors; instead, he suggests that the *Odyssey* is the product of the poet's declining years. Nevertheless, the *Odyssey* is still a great poem: "I am describing an old age, but the old age of *Homer*."

As for Sappho, "Do you not marvel how she seeks to gather soul and body into one, hearing and tongue, eyes and complexion; all dispersed and strangers before: now, by a series of contradictions, she is cold at once and burns, is irrational, is sensible....so that it may not appear to be a single passion that is upon her, but an assemblage of passions?"[31]

The characterizations of Plato, Cicero, and Demosthenes are exciting as are many in Longinus. "In richest abundance, like a very sea, Plato often pours into an open expanse of grandeur.... Cicero and Demosthenes differ in their grand passages. Demosthenes' strength is in sheer height of sublimity, that of Cicero in its diffusion. Our countryman, because he burns and ravages all in his violence, swift, strong, terrible, may be compared to a lightning flash or a thunderbolt. Cicero, like a spreading conflagration, ranges and rolls over the whole field..."[32]

Longinus goes on to suggest that anyone who wishes to attain the sublime should ask himself how Homer, Plato, Demosthenes, or Thucydides would have said the same thing. Subsequently, he passes on to the "artificial" aids. This portion contains little that is novel except for a wonderful digression that shows how the writer without faults never attains the sublime. Homer nods, but he is far superior to Apollonius of Rhodes; this is paralleled in the cases of Demosthenes and Hyperides, Plato and Lysias, Ion and Sophocles. Sublimity is to be preferred to faultlessness. Parenthetically, the younger Pliny touches on the same subject in one of his letters[33] in which he speaks of an orator

whose only fault is that he has none; the orator should strive to soar to
great heights even though by so doing he courts the peril of tumidity.
Cicero and Demosthenes were bold and daring, and ambition forces
Pliny to emulate them in this regard.

Longinus ends his discourse with a few words on the decline of
greatness in literature. The victory of despotism over democracy, he
says, is not the explanation for this decadence, but rather greed,
corruption, love of pleasure, and indolence have withered all greatness
of soul.

In his scores of lectures Dio Chrysostom covered too much ground
to be able to speak with knowledge or even common sense on every
occasion, but once in a while he hit the mark, and he was undeniably at
his best in the twelfth, or Olympic, discourse. This oration was first
given at Olympia itself late in the first century A.D. Perhaps because he
had just been bitten by philosophy or because he felt that the occasion
demanded a little more effort, Dio managed to say something
worthwhile. Not only was his subject, Zeus, appropriate to the place,
but also his treatment of it was fresh and new.

After an introduction that would be a disgrace to any after-dinner
speaker, past or present, Dio finally hit his stride. The beauty and order
of the universe, he said, gave man his first notion of the creator and
ruler of it. This was a mystery that was not revealed in a shrine, but in
the world itself. The first knowledge which man acquired of the
supreme divinity was therefore almost innate. Subsequently this was
amplified through poetry, law, and philosophy, but still another source
of knowledge or concept of Zeus was to be found in the visual
representation provided by painting and sculpture. The artist derived
his own personal concepts from the myths and the poets, but he usually
contributed ideas of his own as well.

At Olympia was the great seated figure of Zeus, the work of Phidias
from which all men now derived their visual image of the god. What
would Phidias say if he were asked to prove that his statue fittingly
portrayed the ruler of gods and men? Pausanias tells us[34] and Dio
implies that there were innumerable statues of Zeus at Olympia. Why
was that of Phidias superior to the others? Dio then allows Phidias
himself to speak. The sculptor argues that the conventional image of
Zeus had already been formed long before his own times; Homer as well
as the earlier sculptors had created a concept which he did not have the
power to alter, and it was only because of his superior technique in
sculpture that he was able to improve upon his predecessors. Nevertheless, mind and intelligence, the essence of the divinity, no sculptor or
painter will ever be able to represent. By providing the deity with a

human form as a vessel to contain intelligence and rationality, something invisible and not capable of portrayal is made visible and comprehensible through a symbol. Phidias has merely done his best, but he does not have the resources of the poet. Poetry is more versatile and can express all the thoughts of the soul and all concepts of shape, action, emotion, or magnitude. Sculpture, on the other hand, is dependent on the workman's tools and the creative touch of the artist. The statue itself is made of durable material, and the sculptor is limited to a single immovable pose which must encompass all that the artist wishes to convey, once and for all, about his subject. The sculptor must create and keep this image in his mind for many years until the work is finished. The poet does not suffer these limitations, and furthermore the eyes are harder to convince than the ears. This statue does not, can not, represent Zeus in all the aspects under which he is worshipped by man. Here in Olympia he is the mild and majestic god, the giver of life and blessings, the common father, saviour, and guardian of all mankind. The statue is composed of the best available material, for what tools of mortal man can work fire, air, and water? Only the god himself can perform such miracles.

From the comparatively Olympian heights of Dio's Olympic Discourse the descent is a long one to the subterranean levels where most art critics lurked in this period. Plutarch[35] had read somewhere that painting is an imitative art like poetry; he alaborated on this by saying that a painting should be admired as a likeness, not as a thing of beauty, since imitation was to be commended as imitation rather than taken seriously as good or bad. Philostratus the Elder[36] defined painting as imitation by the use of colors, but the other Philostratus, Flavius, who wrote the life of Apollonius of Tyana, had something more significant to say. Two relevant passages from his work may be summarized as follows:

In the first,[37] there is a record of a conversation between Apollonius and a painter named Damis. The latter defines painting as imitation by the use of colors, but Apollonius challenges this and points out that monochrome sketches and works of sculpture are also imitative, and that it is also possible "to make likenesses with the mind alone." Furthermore, the mimetic faculty is necessary not only for the creator of a work of art but also for the viewer of such works: "no one could appreciate or admire a picture of a horse or of a bull, unless he had formed an idea of the creature represented." To be more explicit, could one fully appreciate the painting of Timomachus depicting the madness of Ajax unless he knew that, after slaying the flocks of Troy, Ajax would meditate suicide?

In the second passage[38] Apollonius is engaged in a discussion with an Egyptian named Thepesion. Apollonius is somewhat critical of the animal gods of Egypt and arouses the anger of Thepesion who asks ironically whether Phidias and Praxiteles went up to heaven to make sketches of the gods before commencing their figures of Zeus and Aphrodite. Apollonius replies that these works were made by imagination, "a wiser and subtler artist by far than imitation." Imitation can only create what it has seen, but imagination what it has not seen. "If you would fashion an image of Athena you must image in your mind armies and cunning, and handicrafts, and how she leapt out of Zeus himself."

This was the notion, then, of the creative imagination that would idealize the real, "unhampered by the limitations of the imitative process."[39] In the Neo-Platonic system, as opposed to the Aristotelian, imagination, and not imitation, would be the key to the fine arts. By the fourth century another Philostratus would be saying "a certain element of imagination is common to painting and poetry."[40]

Most of the other authors who wrote about or mentioned sculpture or painting had little to contribute in the way of criticism. Pausanias, though he gave the location of hundreds of paintings and works of sculpture, rarely provided a description and almost never an opinion. The miserable *Variae Historiae* of Aelian has more than a dozen anecdotes about painters and sculptors, but this material is absolutely worthless, nor is Athenaeus much better in this regard. The value of what Pliny the Elder has preserved from his reading and copying of earlier authors is very great for the history of art;[41] his own contribution is negligible and reveals little or nothing about criticism in his own day. Pliny says that art has declined because artists, like everyone else, are only interested in making money. Progress, he says, has been achieved in technique and audacity, but that is all. Pliny himself was very partial to a life-like bronze statue of a dog licking itself. He also mentioned the colossal Nero of Zenodorus and its astounding preliminary model in clay. There was in addition an equally colossal painted portrait of the same emperor, one hundred and twenty feet in length, which was struck by lightning. What really impressed Pliny was a painting of Athena by Famulus: the eyes followed you wherever you went!

It is an understatement to say that the *Imagines* of the elder Philostratus will disappoint the reader who seeks to learn about ancient painting or what people thought about it. Philostratus was the son-in-law of the Flavius Philostratus who composed biographies of the sophists and the life of Apollonius of Tyana. When Arthur Fairbanks[42] remarked that no reader can forget that Philostratus the Elder is a sophist, he expressed an opinion not likely to be challenged for a good long time. The sixty-five paintings mentioned in the discourse of Philostratus are just so many springboards for rhetorical high-diving. It is only in a few instances that he provides even the barest description of the painting under discussion, but some of the passages are of interest.

On one occasion, Philostratus points out that perspective is used in a siege scene: some of the figures are shown in full, others with legs hidden; of others, only the heads or helmets are visible. The purpose of perspective, says Philostratus, is to deceive the eyes as they travel back along the receding planes of the picture. In the portrait of Narcissus, "the arm shows an open space at the point where the elbow bends, a wrinkle where the wrist is twisted, and it casts a shadow as it ends in the palm of the hand." He is impressed by the picture of Pelops in which the artist has shown four horses together, yet he has not confused "their several legs with another." He admires the shading of the *Atlas,* "for the shadows on a crouching figure like his run into one another, and they do not darken any of the projecting parts but they produce light on the parts that are hollow and retreating." Occasionally, the symbolism of a picture is explained as in the picture of the marsh where the male date palm tree has stretched out in an attempt to embrace a female of the species.

As he describes the picture entitled *The Islands,* Philostratus must be consciously imitating Homer's *Shield of Achilles.* The wealth of detail which *The Islands* obviously contained reminds us of the work of Polygnotos which Pausanias[43] described at such length in one of the few cases where he bothered to describe anything. The picture discussed by Philostratus, however, was no great masterpiece but rather belonged in the landscape category like the murals of Studius so admired by Pliny the Elder.[44]

Good things in scholarship and criticism were certainly few and far between in the era of the Pax Romana. Perhaps it was too much to expect teachers to be scholars or to hope that the acrobats of the lecture platform could supply important criticism. As far as sculpture and painting were concerned, the popular ideal was mimesis just as it had been for many centuries. What was more to be desired than photographic painting or a statue like Pygmalion's that would come to life? One recalls uneasily that the *Greek Anthology* contains one epigram on the *Zeus* of Phidias and thirty-two on Myron's marvelous *Heifer,* which fooled even the bulls!

FOOTNOTES

1. Pliny, *Letters*, III, 5.

2. Galen, *On Habits*, 11. Translated by A. J. Brock, *Greek Medicine*, London 1929, p. 185. Reprinted by permission of E. P. Dutton & Co., Inc., New York.

3. R. Walzer, *Galen on Jews and Christians*, Oxford 1949, p. 75.

4. Aulus Gellius, *Attic Nights*, Preface 2. Reprinted by permission of the publishers from J. C. Rolfe, *Aulus Gellius, Attic Nights*, Cambridge, Mass.: Harvard University Press, 1930.

5. W. R. Roberts, *Demetrius on Style*, (Loeb Classical Texts) London and New York 1927, pp. 282-287.

6. W. R. Roberts, *Dionysius of Halicarnassus: The Three Literary Letters*, Cambridge 1901, Letter to Pompeius.

7. Aulus Gellius, *Attic Nights*, II, 5.

8. W. R. Roberts, *Dionysius of Halicarnassus on Literary Composition*, London 1910, pp. 95-96. See also S. F. Bonner, *Literary Treatises of Dionysius of Halicarnassus*, Cambridge, 1939.

9. J.W. H. Atkins, *Literary Criticism in Antiquity*, Cambridge 1934, Vol. II, pp. 347-8; see also J. D. Deniston, *Greek Literary Criticism*, London 1924, p. ix.

10. H. Nettleship, "Literary Criticism in Latin Antiquity," *Lectures and Essays*, Second Series, London 1895, p. 72.

11. Aulus Gellius, *Attic Nights*, I, 21; V, 81; IX, 9; XIII, 27. See also Suetonius, *Life of Virgil*.

12. Fronto to Marcus Aurelius (Naber, p. 155) translated by C. R. Haines, *Marcus Cornelius Fronto* (Loeb Classical Texts) London and New York 1920, II, p. 105.

13. Quintilian, *Institutes*, X, 1, 125.

14. Aulus Gellius, *Attic Nights*, XV, 24.

15. Nettleship, *op. cit.*, p. 90; Atkins, *op. cit.*, pp. 195-6.

16. Nettleship, *op. cit.*, p. 90.

17. Atkins, *op. cit.*, pp. 178-196.

18. Tacitus, *Dialogus*, 5.

19. Petronius, *Satyricon*, 118.

20. Nettleship, *op. cit.*, pp. 84-85.

21. Atkins, *op. cit.*, pp. 300-301.

22. Cassius Dio, *Epitome*, 69, 4.

23. Reprinted by permission of the publishers from C. R. Haines, *Marcus Cornelius Fronto*, Cambridge, Mass.: Harvard University Press, 1919. The passage is from Vol. I, p. 141.

24. *Ibid.*, II, p. 103.

25. The text may be found in H. G. Evelyn-White, *Hesiod*, (Loeb Classical Texts) London and Cambridge 1943, p. 567 ff.

26. Aulus Gellius, *Attic Nights*, III, 11.

27. Pack, *Literary Papyri*, p. 44.

28. L. Cooper, *An Aristotelian Theory of Comedy*, New York 1922.

29. Demetrius, *On Style*, III, 165.

30. Quintilian, *Institutes*, VI, 3, 14.

31. Extract taken from A. O. Prickard, *Longinus on the Sublime*, Oxford 1949, pp. 23-24 by permission of the Clarendon Press, Oxford. The same permission applies to the passage immediately following (footnote 32).

32. *Ibid.*, p. 88.

33. Pliny, *Letters*, IX, 26.

34. Pausanias, *Description of Greece*, V, 1, 22.

35. Plutarch, *How a Young Man should read Poetry*, 17.

36. Philostratus, *Imagines*, Preface 1.

37. Philostratus, *Apollonius of Tyana*, II, 22.

38. *Ibid.*, VI, 19.

39. Atkins, *op. cit.*, II, p. 344.

40. Philostratus, *Imagines*, 391 K.

41. For his sources, see E. Sellers, *The Elder Pliny's Chapters on the History of Art*, London 1896.

42. *Philostratus the Elder*, (Loeb Classical Texts) London and New York 1931, p. xxi.

43. Pausanias, *Description of Greece*, X, 25-31.

44. Pliny, *Natural History*, XXXV, 1, 116-117.

Philosophers and Philosophists

Here is one man milking a billy-goat, and another catching the proceeds in a sieve.

Demonax

He lived to the age of fifty-eight and died leaving a child who was legitimate but uneducated.

Epitaph for a Sophist

WHEN ONE DISCOVERS so many people striving, or being exhorted, to be or to become good, it is difficult to believe that Rome under the Pax Romana was suffering moral decline. The well-intentioned Plutarch, the saintly Marcus Aurelius, the reformed Dio, Epictetus the revivalist, and even the charlatan Apollonius of Tyana were all on the right side when it came to ethics; Seneca talked a good game, too. Among the prominent philosophers of the age, the preaching of morality was their principal stock in trade. The basic "science" that underlay the systems of the various schools of philosophy was still taught half-heartedly and hurriedly, and some teachers dwelt on dialectic, but most, like Seneca,[1] preferred to play down the "natural" and "rational" and to amplify instead upon the "moral." The prevailing neglect of the first two elements was probably what Seneca had in mind and approved when he said that what had once been philosophy had become scholarship. Epictetus shunned dialectic and almost never discussed science.[2]

The desire for goodness and the persuasiveness of the great teachers, or preachers, was such that some people were actually "converted" to philosophy and reformed their lives in essentially the same way that many of their neighbors and fellow townsmen were being converted to Christianity during this very period. Conversion, the reorientation of the soul,[3] was not the only thing that the adherents of philosophy and the Christians had in common. Certain words, phrases, similes, metaphors, symbols, and concepts served one group as well as the other. The similarities were so frequent and striking that it is hard to know whether they would attract or repel the prospective convert to Christianity. On the one hand, a pagan would not feel himself in

unfamiliar territory; on the other hand, he might be disappointed that
so little was really new in this new religion.

St. Paul said, "Wherein thou judgest another, thou condemnest
thyself"; Epictetus said, "What have you to do with another man's evil?
Your own evil is to make a bad defence; only guard against that, but
just as being condemned or not condemned is another's function, so it
is another's evil." "We glory in tribulations" is matched by Seneca's
"Disaster is virtue's opportunity.... gold is tried by fire; brave men by
misfortune." "Know ye not that they which run in a race run all, but
only one receiveth the prize" and the ideas associated with it find a
parallel many times in the agonistic similes of Epictetus, as, for
example, "It is an Olympic contest in which you are intending to enter
your name...." The "Let every soul be subject unto the higher
powers.... render therefore to all their dues" appears in Epictetus as,
"Do you philosophers, then, teach us to despise our kings?... Far from
it. Who among us teaches you to dispute their claim to the things over
which they have authority?" The many parallels between St. Paul and
Seneca are well known,[4] and the later Christians, when the battle
between their faith and paganism had long since ended, recognized the
community of ideas which they shared with the philosophers. A typical
attitude was that of the good metropolitan of Euchaita who felt that
Plutarch was a Christian and did not know it.[5]

In addition to its emphasis on morality and its general avoidance of
science and dialectic, philosophy under the Pax Romana was characterized by a strong tendency toward eclecticism. The traditional schools —
Platonic, Peripatetic, Stoic, and Epicurean — still had their representatives; there were also people who called themselves Cynics or
Pythagoreans; but the individual philosophies were seldom adopted in a
pure form. The Romans, as everyone knows, were most attracted to
Stoicism. Seneca, Epictetus, and Marcus Aurelius regarded themselves
as Stoics, but Seneca showed Platonic and Skeptic influences, Epictetus
leaned toward Cynicism, and there was much of Epicurus in the
Meditations. Dio was officially a Cynic; and Galen, a Peripatetic; both
agreed in opposing the Epicureans and were joined in this by Seneca
and Epictetus, but Dio and Galen leaned heavily on Plato. Plutarch,
sometimes called the first Neo-Platonist, belonged more to the school
of Plato than to any other although even he was an eclectic.[6] Lucian,
though anti-Cynic and pro-Epicurean, was so thoroughly imbued with
skepticism that he was never identified with any school.

The philosopher's philosopher, according to Epictetus, was the
Cynic. Imitation Cynics were plentiful enough; an outstanding example
was the friend of Athenaeus who advertised his persuasion by always

appearing in public with two big white dogs and whose home was a veritable kennel. Dirty clothes, long hair and beards, poverty, opposition to authority, and general churlishness marked these synthetic Cynics. There were few genuine Cynics, like Lucian's Demonax. As a matter of fact, it is hard to understand how people have been able to see in Demonax anything but a figment of Lucian's fertile imagination. Demetrius, "that barking dog" of the Flavian period, was real enough,[7] but he lacked the wit and wisdom of Lucian's second century Bernard Baruch whose stone bench in Athens became a public shrine. Demonax, said Lucian, admired Socrates, Diogenes, and Aristippus; their lives as presented by Diogenes Laertius when compared with Lucian's life of Demonax will show that Lucian was well acquainted with the popular stories which were told about this philosophical triumvirate.

Although Philostratus was no more reliable as a philosophical biographer than Lucian, he at least wrote in earnest and chose a real person for his subject. The hero of Philostratus, and apparently of many others, was Apollonius of Tyana, a Neopythagorean who flourished in the second half of the first century. This Proteus reborn, who had been an Egyptian pilot in one of his previous reincarnations, was a vegetarian and a teetotaler. After he had completed a self-imposed silence of five years, he was ever afterwards a hard man to shut up; he talked in turn and out of turn and even reappeared almost two centuries after his death to talk the Emperor Aurelian out of destroying Tyana.[8] The travels of Apollonius encompassed the earth. He went to Babylon; he saw the wonders of India including some gold-digging griffins; he preached at Ephesus, Smyrna, Athens, and other Greek towns; he interviewed the ghost of Achilles at Troy; he was in Rome at least twice and also visited Spain, Egypt, and the source of the Nile. An opponent of the tyrants, Nero and Domitian, he was the confidant and adviser of several better, if not good, emperors, Vespasian, Titus, and Nerva. Apollonius possessed the gift of tongues; he even learned to speak the language of birds. To his powers of divination, he added the power of healing; in a pinch, he could even raise the dead. Apollonius was a thorn in the throne of Domitian; he not only bested the tyrant in an argument but also vanished from the room after his victory so that Domitian was unable to provide the reward reserved for such occasions. Later on, by means of some variety of built-in television peculiar to himself, Apollonius while in Ephesus witnessed the murder of Domitian as it occurred in Rome.[9] The Christians knew all about Apollonius, but he was one philosopher they did not wish to claim; they hotly denied the soterial parallels alleged by the pagans.[10]

What the real Apollonius was like, we may never know, but his career was sufficiently spectacular to encourage some imitation. Lucian has a story about a certain Alexander of Abonutichus who was a prophet false in several ways. We cannot trust Lucian for the details, but the existence of Alexander and the cult which he founded have been tentatively confirmed by numismatic and archaeological evidence. Alexander was, like Apollonius, a species of Pythagorean who practised divination. His profitable business in oracles was supplemented by a little judicious blackmail on the side.

Still another racketeer was Proteus or Peregrine who was admired by Aulus Gellius but who made a less favorable impression on Lucian. Proteus was a Christian apostate who became a Cynic. After he wore out his welcome in Athens by frequent criticism of Herodes Atticus and by subversive activity against the Roman government, he tried to recover his lost prestige with a publicity stunt. Proteus went to the Olympic festival where he made it known that he would publicly cremate himself in order to demonstrate the way in which one should despise death. As Lucian tells the story, Proteus expected that the bystanders would restrain him at the last moment; but instead they encouraged him to proceed with his plan. By that time there was no turning back, and the unfortunate man had no choice but to cast himself into the flames.

It is a relief to turn from these unwashed — even Apollonius of Tyana was averse to bathing — and quarrelsome exhibitionists to the Stoics who, even if they were no great shakes at philosophy, were at least socially acceptable. Most of the Stoics seem to have been earnest enough and, like most preachers, they somewhat compensated for their lack of brain power by their sincerity and general decency. Seneca, though a Stoic, may be excluded from consideration; he was neither sincere nor decent as the *Apocolocyntosis* clearly shows.

Pliny the Younger and Epictetus were impressed by the Stoic Euphrates who flourished at Rome in the Age of the Flavians. Euphrates possessed a wonderful bedside manner; he was polite, affable, and willing to take or fake an interest in the problems of others. Pliny had met him out in Syria and cultivated his acquaintance later on in Rome. Tall, handsome, with long hair and a huge white beard, Euphrates had all the attributes of a society philosopher. Both Pliny, quite naturally, and Epictetus, rather strangely, were impressed by Euphrates' considerable oratorical talents. Epictetus remarked that when some people had seen and heard a philosopher like Euphrates, they wished to be philosophers themselves. Euphrates claimed that he tried to conceal his profession as a philosopher; in some way, however, people seemed to be able to penetrate his disguise. Philostratus reported a bitter feud between Apollonius of Tyana and Euphrates; the latter was seeking Vespasian's patronage during the revolt against Vitellius and did not want Apollonius for a competitor. It was said that Euphrates urged Vespasian, if he managed to overthrow Vitellius, to restore the republic, while Apollonius very sensibly pointed out that the republic was dead and the principate a reality. Euphrates lived to a ripe old age and finally committed suicide by drinking hemlock, with express imperial permission, early in the reign of Hadrian.

The teacher of Epictetus, Musonius Rufus, a Stoic with Cynic propensities, was something of a social misfit when compared with the suave Euphrates. The latter would have adorned a china shop, while Musonius frequently behaved like the proverbial bull. Hard headed and uncompromising in his teaching, Musonius objected to the custom of applauding a lecture, saying that it turned the whole affair into a flute player's recital. This remark and others like it made to students, as well as his maxims, were treasured and quoted long after his death. Outside the classroom Musonius Rufus was not so much in his element. He was expelled from Rome for political agitation and put into a labor gang digging Nero's ill-fated Corinth canal. He was nearly mobbed by the Athenians when he objected to gladiatorial games in the Theatre of Dionysus. Later, when Vitellius appointed him to an embassy empowered to treat with the forces of Vespasian, Musonius seized the opportunity to harangue the soldiers on the benefits of peace and the perils of war, and once again he barely escaped with his life. Musonius' other extravagances included a kind of Brook Farm experiment and his advocacy of philosophical studies for women.

Arrian's stenographic record of the diatribes of Epictetus as well as his *Encheiridion* are the fullest accounts of that eminent teacher which have survived. Marcus Aurelius frequently quotes Epictetus, but his source, like that of Aulus Gellius, was probably Arrian. One of the maxims of Epictetus, "Bear and Forbear," was a favorite quotation. This epitomized very nicely the teaching of Epictetus, although it has been suggested that "Endure and Renounce" might better express the true thought.[11] The warmth and humanity of Epictetus arouse a feeling of congeniality that is lacking in the turncoat Seneca, the smooth Euphrates, or the bullheaded Musonius. God, said Epictetus, brought man into the world to be a spectator and interpreter of his works. It is no simple task, the fulfilling of the profession of a man. The beginning of philosophy is a consciousness of man's own weakness. What is the object of virtue? Serenity. "Do not seek to have everything happen as you wish, but wish for everything to happen as it actually does, and then you will achieve serenity." "We must be like those who are playing at ball; we are not concerned whether the ball is good or bad, but only about throwing and catching it."

There is a fine passage in the *Encheiridion:*[12]

> Just as on a voyage, when your ship has anchored, if you should go on shore to get fresh water, you may pick up a small shellfish or a little bulb on the way, but you have to keep your attention fixed on the ship and turn about frequently for fear lest the captain should call; and if he calls, you must give up all these things, if you would escape being thrown on board all tied up like a sheep. So it is also in life: if there be given you, instead of a little bulb and a small shellfish, a little wife and child, there will be no objection to that; only, if the Captain calls, give up all these things and run to the ship, without even turning around to look back. And if you are an old man, never even get very far away from the ship, for fear that when He calls you may be missing.

Marcus Aurelius often quotes Epictetus directly; sometimes there is a paraphrase, and there are many similes and metaphors common to both. The phrase "citizen of the world" is a great favorite. The simile of the actor is also used several times. Says Epictetus:[13] "Remember that you are an actor in a play, the character of which is determined by the Playwright; if He wishes the play to be short, it is short; if long, it is long." Marcus ended his *Meditations* by saying that nature, which brought man into the world, also ordered his departure from it in the way that a praetor might dismiss an actor from the stage; it did not matter if only three of the five acts had been completed, for "in life the three acts are the whole drama; for what shall be a complete play is determined by Him who was once the cause of its composition, and now of its dissolution.... Depart therefore satisfied, for He who releases you also is satisfied."[14]

Marcus Aurelius, like most of his educated contemporaries, was a great notetaker. Aulus Gellius and Galen tell us that they did the same thing. In a letter to Fronto, Marcus mentioned filling five notebooks in a few days with his gleanings from "sixty volumes." The disorganization of the *Meditations* and the many passages cited from Epictetus, Plato, and others as well as the sections which can be attributed to his sources by a comparison of the texts, help us to see that the work is not a treatise on philosophy; rather, it is a collection from Marcus scrapbooks which he continued to compile almost to the end of his life. Marcus may have attained goodness through philosophy, but his studies never freed him from the haunting fear of death. His searchings only increased his skepticism in the philosophical sense. We do not know how the teachers felt about the serenity which they said was attainable, but the *Meditations* show that at least one student might have been much happier with the positive assurances that Christianity could provide.

Hortative philosophy was perhaps the kind most likely to flourish in an age which was dominated by rhetoric. Fair sounding phrases were more attractive than closely woven arguments. Epictetus and others were probably right when they told their students that it was not essential to be able to understand Chrysippus, yet this attitude was a symptom of decline: people did not want to think. Epictetus, in inveighing against the Academy, insisted that it was necessary to accept a self-evident truth even though you could prove it was false. The philosophers of the Pax Romana did not talk about faith as the Christians did, but faith was just as essential to the attainment of goodness as it was to becoming a true Christian.

There was skepticism not only within but also without philosophy. Lucian in his *Hermotimus* and Galen on several occasions stressed the matter which was most damaging to the prestige of philosophy: the philosophers could not agree and were continually at war among themselves. Dio sadly confessed that the philosophers of his day were owls, reputed to be wise but in reality the most stupid of birds. People were like the birds who flocked around the owl; when they saw a man dressed like a philosopher, they gathered around him. "And so," said Dio, "we, like the owls, collect a great company of those who are in truth birds, being fools ourselves besides being annoyed by others of a like folly."[15] During the reign of Marcus Aurelius, the philosopher emperor, it became fashionable to take up philosophy since an imperial owl had been substituted for a regal eagle. Apuleius fondly imagined himself a philosopher, and advertised himself as one, but he was really a walking encyclopedia of an inferior kind.

Whether they attained perfection or helped others to do so, many teachers of philosophy were loved and long remembered by their students. Musonius and Epictetus were outstanding in this regard, and Sextus, the nephew of Plutarch, was so highly venerated by Marcus Aurelius that he found association with him "more agreeable than any flattery." Aulus Gellius often spoke with real affection of the Platonist Taurus, a pupil of Plutarch, with whom he studied in Athens.

In his reminiscences of student days in Athens Aulus Gellius gives us little pictures of life in an ancient university town. In the classes of Taurus the students would read together the dialogues of Plato and the commentaries on them. Taurus would lecture daily using the "books of the ancients" and his own commentaries; after the lecture there was always a question period. Often Taurus would invite the students to his home for a supper that invariably consisted of a pot of beans embellished with gourds cut into small pieces. Each guest was supposed to make a contribution to the affair by bringing a "light problem" to be discussed after the meal. Aulus remembered a few of these: When did a man learning an art become an artist? When did a rising man rise? When he stood up or was still seated? Taurus insisted that these discussions were worthwhile, for he said that this group of problems, for example, illustrated Plato's "moment of sudden separation" as presented in the *Parmenides*.

Aulus was a member of a group of young Romans who all had the same teachers and attended the same lectures. As foreign students, they tended to stick together. When it came time for the Saturnalia, they decided to celebrate the ancient Roman festival "merrily but temperately." They arranged a dinner party and devised a game in which the host posed a series of questions, one for each guest, and determined the order of speaking by lot. When a question was correctly answered, the prize was a crown and a manuscript of some Greek or Roman writer. Among the questions were "an obscure saying of some early poet, amusing rather than perplexing; some point in ancient history; the correction of some tenet of philosophy which was commonly misinterpreted, the solution of some sophistical catch, the investigation of a rare and unusual word, or of an obscure use of the tense of a very of plain meaning." The game was so popular that they used to play it at the baths by discussing catch questions called "sophisms." A throw of the dice indicated which man was to solve and refute the sophistry under discussion. If he failed, he was fined a sestertius, and the money thus collected was used to finance subsequent dinner parties.

When Apollonius of Tyana visited Athens, he landed at the Piraeus and on his way up to the city met large numbers of students bound for Phalerum. "Some of them were stripped, for in autumn the sun is hot upon the Athenians; and others were studying books, and some were rehearsing their speeches, and others were disputing."[16] Apollonius was soon recognized; the students crowded around him; he greeted them cordially and congratulated them on their study of philosophy.

Not everyone came to Athens as a student to "major" in philosophy, for the town was also a center for rhetorical studies as well as a Mecca for sophists. Oratory had long been a study of importance at Athens. Then, when the chairs of rhetoric and philosophy with their handsome salaries were established there in the second century, aspirants flocked to the town and waited for the incumbent professors to die so that they might contend for their positions. St. Paul fully recognized the special nature of the audience he would have to face in Athens; his speech delivered on the Areopagus shows the most careful preparation.

Not for five hundred years had the sophists enjoyed the fame and adulation that was theirs in the first and second centuries A.D. Despite their not infrequent claims to universal knowledge, these latter-day sophists would have been no match in originality, versatility, or learning for the sophists of the fifth century B.C. The luminaries of the Second Sophistic were primarily rhetoricians and platform entertainers, Chautauqua lecturers, but they provided their audiences with the pyrotechnics that the schools had trained them to admire. Some of the sophists had famous speeches which were delivered over and over to audiences throughout the length and breadth of the empire; William Jennings Bryan and his "Cross of Gold" constitute the closest modern parallel to these performances. A variation on this practice was to speak several times on the same theme without repeating what had been said before; still another sophistic trick was to allow the audience to pick a theme and then speak extemporaneously on it. Public contests between two or more sophists were also very popular.

Many, perhaps most, of the sophists were teachers as well as lecturers, but seldom have professors enjoyed so much prestige and authority outside the classroom as well as in it. They rode roughshod over municipal officials, Roman governors, and even some of the emperors themselves. When a man named Apollonius was invited to tutor the young Caesar Marcus Aurelius at the palace, he replied that he would prefer Marcus to come to him at his house. We can thus appreciate more fully what is meant when Marcus says in the *Meditations*, "From Apollonius I learned freedom of will." When Antoninus Pius was proconsul of Asia and took up quarters for the night in the house of Polemo in Smyrna, the sophist arrived home unexpectedly at midnight and forced the future emperor to find other lodgings. Adrian of Tyre was possessed of almost unbearable egotism. When he was appointed to the chair of rhetoric at Athens, he commenced his inaugural lecture with the words, "Once again letters have come from Phoenicia!" Many of the sophists were unpleasant in other ways: Philagrus of Cilicia quarreled with everyone he met, often on the slightest pretext; he admitted that he was so bad tempered that he did not even enjoy himself. Among many famous or notorious eccentrics were the uncouth Marcus of Byzantium, Alexander the "Clay-Plato" who was elegant, vacuous, and reputed to be the son of

Apollonius of Tyana, and Varus "the Stork" whose prominent beaked nose had a fiery hue.

The epitome of all sophism in the second century was that same Polemo who successfully bullied Antoninus Pius. His supremacy was admitted even by Herodes Atticus, himself no mean sophist; Herodes was said to have paid him 250,000 drachmae for a single speech. The *skene*, or platform manner, of Polemo was regarded as very effective: his calm, easy smile as he rounded off a period demonstrated how simple these things were for a master; sometimes he would jump to his feet to emphasize a point, or, in moments of tension, paw the ground like a horse. Although he was not born at Smyrna, Polemo took up his residence there and was politically influential in the town and in all Ionia for many years. A crippling disease prevented him from being a great traveler, although he did visit Athens and Rome; he died in middle age, fighting to the very end and crying, "Give me a body, and I will declaim."

The Asianic style of Polemo did not always hit the mark at first. Herodes confessed that it grew on one, and Marcus Aurelius was not at all impressed when he heard Polemo for the first time. Marcus wrote to Fronto that Polemo was a hardworking farmer who was in the business for profit rather than pleasure. Dionysius of Miletus, though he later changed his mind, was not bowled over by his first exposure to Polemo either; he commented, "This athlete possesses strength, but it does not come from the wrestling ground." Apparently, Dionysius, who had had a great deal of forensic experience, thought this seasoning was lacking in Polemo.

Not all the sophists lived in Athens; they were abundant in Rome. The teacher of Dionysius of Miletus, and also of Marcus of Byzantium and Lollianus, was the Assyrian Isaeus who was known to Juvenal[17] and Pliny the Younger.[18] Pliny expressed great admiration for Isaeus. He admired his Attic style and his facility in extemporaneous speaking. Isaeus would offer several topics and leave the choice up to the audience even to the point of allowing them to name the side of the argument to be taken. Pliny remarked on the exceptional mnemonic powers of Isaeus, for the man could repeat word for word the extemporaneous speech which he had just given. Isaeus was credited by others with having developed some exotic Chaldean system of memorization which he imparted to his pupils.

Regarded as a philosopher by the sophists and a sophist by the philosophers was Favorinus of Arelate, the friend of Plutarch, Fronto and Aulus Gellius. Although Favorinus came from Gaul and was educated in Rome, Greek rather than Latin was his special language. He was reputed to have written many books on history, philosophy, and geography, including a ten-volume affair on "Pyrronian principles." If there was anything Favorinus did not know, he was not quick to admit it. Aulus Gellius quotes Favorinus as his authority on Socrates, literary style, etymology, medicine, judicial procedure, science, grammar, Sallust, dialectic, legal history, and physiology. He knew all about gynecology, and his practical knowledge was so extensive that he once advised a lady on how to nurse her baby. Obviously an opinionated fellow, Favorinus did not believe in astrology.

The influence of Favorinus was very considerable. He was mentioned far more often by his contemporaries than any of his fellow sophists with the possible exception of Dio whom Favorinus claimed as his teacher although no one could see that Dio had had much influence upon his pupil. The so-called thirty-seventh discourse of Dio appears to be an oration of Favorinus delivered at Corinth, and another one of Favorinus' speeches has been found on a papyrus school text dating from the third century. Two other third century papyri confirm the fact that Favorinus had become a school author.[19]

In this quarrelsome age, an eminent man could not expect to win universal approbation. Polemo did not care much for Favorinus; he referred to him as an old woman. Hadrian did not always see eye to eye with Favorinus, either; it was even said that Hadrian tried to overthrow both Favorinus and Dionysius of Miletus by favoring their rivals.[20] It is sure that Favorinus temporarily fell from imperial favor when he was accused of adultery with the wife of a consul; at this time, the Athenians and possibly the Corinthians overturned the statues which they had erected to Favorinus, yet he managed to weather the storm and recover some of his prestige. He himself used to say that his life was distinguished by three paradoxes: though a Gaul, he led the life of a Hellene; though he had quarreled with the emperor, he was still alive; though a eunuch, he had been tried for adultery. Lucian was no admirer of Favorinus. The satire, the *Eunuch,* was obviously aimed at Favorinus although it was composed several years after his death. The humor, as might be anticipated, was a little broad, but it was better sustained in this satirical dialogue than in some of Lucian's other compositions which often ended rather weakly.

One of the distinctions of Favorinus was that he was able to count Herodes Atticus among his students. Herodes, through his Athenian citizenship, his immense wealth, and his unquestioned ability, became one of the most important of the sophists not only as a performer but also as a teacher and the leader of a movement away from the florid Asianic and back to the Attic style. Linked with the imperial family by ancient ties of friendship, Herodes also tutored Marcus Aurelius in Greek oratory. He served the Roman imperial government in various capacities and crowned his official career with the consulship. Aulus Gellius remembered Herodes as a gracious host who, though an orator, was quick to defend philosophy from the pretenders who tried to storm its ramparts. Athens, many towns in Greece, and even cities in Asia Minor were beautified through the generosity of Herodes whose major regret was that he had not been able to realize his greatest dream, the construction of a canal through the Isthmus of Corinth. Rhetorician, scholar, and philanthropist, Herodes Atticus was also regarded as the equal of Pliny the Younger and Marcus Aurelius in epistolography. Despite his prestige, literary attainments, and great wealth, the happiness of his life was marred by the loss of many members of his family and the stupidity of his son who preferred debauchery to sophistry. Herodes was deeply grieved by the death of any member of his family, even of children who were stillborn. He also mourned the deaths of friends and teachers to a degree that seemed excessive; he never attained, and frequently resented, the apathy toward such tragedies that the Stoics professed to have achieved.

Other chinks in the urbanity of Herodes were discovered at an early date. He quarreled with Antoninus Pius when the latter was governor of Asia; some even said that he conspired against Antoninus when he was emperor. The Athenians claimed that Herodes had diddled them out of considerable sums left to them by his father's will. One thing led to another, and the cauldron boiled over: Herodes was accused of many crimes, including the murder of his own wife in whose memory he had built the famous covered theater on the south slope of the Acropolis. The accuser was a man named Demostratus who was able to obtain the advice and assistance of Marcus Cornelius Fronto in conducting the case before the emperor. Marcus Aurelius tried to head Fronto off, but Fronto adopted a most austere attitude. He was determined to let the chips fall in the proverbial manner. Who could imagine that, as the tutor of Marcus Aurelius in Latin oratory, Fronto would be jealous of Herodes, who had instructed Marcus in Greek oratory? Although the speech of Demostratus was to enjoy great fame (or notoriety), Herodes Atticus was acquitted. Twenty years later, a new quarrel developed between Herodes and the Quintilii who were representing the Roman government in the Balkans. This time Herodes, angry and embittered, abandoned his rhetoric and spoke plainly even against what he called the ingratitude of Marcus Aurelius himself. Herodes professed himself ready to die, and, under another emperor, he would have been accommodated, but Marcus dealt kindly with him even to the point of renewing their friendship a few years before Herodes died.

Among the pupils of Herodes, in addition to Marcus Aurelius, were Aristocles, Aristides, Adrian, Chrestus of Byzantium, and Ptolemy of Naucratis. The reputation of Herodes was such that people insisted that he should be numbered among the ten Attic orators along with Demosthenes, Aeschines, and the rest. Herodes was extremely modest about this; he acknowledged the supremacy of all the ten orators except Andocides.[21]

Like Herodes and Polemo, the two greatest orators of the second century, Dio and Aristides, were intimate with emperors and very influential in the affairs of the Greek towns of the empire. Dio worked very hard to alleviate the inter- and intra-city strife of the Bithynian towns, while Aristides was credited with having brought about the rebuilding of Smyrna after a disastrous earthquake. It was said that Trajan was much impressed with Dio although he confessed that he did not understand much of what Dio had to say. Dio was a showman like many of the others; among his "props" was a lion's skin which he used as a costume on appropriate occasions. Aristides was, in the last analysis, a man of many words and few ideas, but he spoke beautifully.

Much dimmer than the lights of the great sophists were those of Pollux, Apuleius, and Aelian. Pollux, the author of the *Onomasticon,* was no rhetorician though he aspired to be one. Philostratus could scarcely find the words to classify him. Lucian was not tongue-tied, however, for he pilloried poor Pollux in two satires, the *Lexiphanes* and the *Professor of Rhetoric.* Apuleius enjoyed a great reputation in North Africa, an area definitely in the bush league. If we possessed only the *Apology* and the *Florida* and lacked the *Metamorphoses,* the name of Apuleius would seldom be mentioned today. As for Aelian, whatever may have been the merits of his prose, he was a compiler of the worst sort. "Simplicity," says Philostratus,[22] "was the prevailing note of his style"; and, we may add, of his thought as well.

The three most distinguished professions, according to Hermogenes,[23] were those of the soldier, the rhetorician, and the philosopher. Three of the Good Emperors attained these heights: Trajan, the soldier; Hadrian, the sophist; and Marcus Aurelius, the philosopher. If these goals were good enough for the rulers, they were adequate for their subjects as well. The measure of the age can justly be taken from the calibre of its sophists and philosophers, for they had attained the ideal toward which many others strove. A Polemo, a Favorinus, or even a Dio left something to be desired, and an age in which a Plutarch was regarded as the ornament and lyre of philosophy was truly in a bad way.[24]

FOOTNOTES

1. Seneca, *Epistles*, 89.

2. Epictetus, *Discourses* (hereafter quoted as *Diatribes*), II, 17, 19; Aulus Gellius, *Attic Nights*, XVII, 19.

3. A. D. Nock, *Conversion*, London 1933, p. 7.

4. For a convenient collection, see J. F. Hurst and H. C. Whiting, *L. Annaeus Seneca*, New York 1877, pp. 40-46.

5. John, Metropolitan of Euchaita, quoted in *Plutarchii Moralia* (Wyttenbach, Oxford 1795-1830), Preface, Chapter III, paragraph 1.

6. R. M. Jones, *Platonism of Plutarch*, Menasha 1916.

7. For Demetrius, see Cassius Dio, *Epitome*, 65, 13; Eunapius, *Lives of the Sophists*, 454; Philostratus, *Sophists*, 42.

8. *Scriptores Historiae Augustae, Aurelian*, XXIV, 3.

9. Cassius Dio, *Epitome*, 67, 18; Philostratus, *Apollonius of Tyana*, VIII, 26.

10. Eusebius, *Against the Life of Apollonius, passim.*

11. W. A. Oldfather, *Epictetus*, (Loeb Classical Texts) London 1926, Vol. I, p. xvii.

12. Epictetus, *Encheiridion*, 7. Reprinted by permission of the publishers from W. A. Oldfather, *Epictetus*, Cambridge, Mass.: Harvard University Press 1925.

13. *Ibid.*, 17.

14. Marcus Aurelius, *Meditations*, XII, 36.

15. Dio, *Seventy-second Discourse*, 16; also *Twelfth Discourse*, 1.

16. Philostratus, *Apollonius of Tyana*, IV, 17.

17. Juvenal, *Satires*, III, 24.

18. Pliny, *Letters*, II, 3.

19. Pack, *Greek and Latin Literary Papyri*, nos. 330, 1559, 1629.

20. *Scriptores Historiae Augustae, Hadrian*, XV, 12; Cassius Dio, *Epitome*, 69, 3; Philostratus, *Sophists*, I, 8.

21. For Herodes, see Philostratus, *Sophists*, II, 1; the letters of Fronto, *passim*, and Aulus Gellius, *Attic Nights*.

22. Philostratus, *Sophists*, II, 31.

23. A. D. Nock, *Sallustius*, Cambridge 1926, p. xviii.

24. Eunapius, *op. cit.*, 454.

Vultures in Gowns

The lowest of the people, the lawyers, beasts of the courts, and advocates that are but vultures in gowns....

Apuleius

SUETONIUS[1] HAS A STORY about an eminent grammarian who appeared as an advocate in a Roman court. Disdainful of legal strategy, the learned man confounded his opponents by vigorously attacking the diction of their lawyer, In desperation the other side finally requested an adjournment until they could hire a pedant of their own.

Although this tale has a certain aura of the incredible, one hesitates to brand it as apochryphal. Roman legal procedure under the early principate had more than its share of marvels. Without history for our witness, if we did not know how Roman law was disciplined and improved by the later principate and the autocracy, it would be difficult to explain how it managed to extricate itself from the quagmire of the first century A.D. Fortunately, it is possible to observe rather closely the situation at its worst under Domitian and Trajan and to see how Hadrian and his successors were able to rescue the law from the wretched state into which it had fallen. An understanding of the matter can be aided at the outset by making some slight distinction between theory and practice.

The golden-tongued Dio, elevated by the warm currents of his own eloquence, once proclaimed that the law was a guide for life, an overseer of cities, the protector of old age, the schoolmaster of youth, the guardian of wealth, and the ally of peace. His more sedate contemporary, the jurist Celsus, defined the law as the art of what is good and fair, while others called it the science of the just and unjust. Ulpian agreed with Dio that the law was a guide for life when he said that its principles were to live uprightly, to injure no man, and to give every man his due.

Accustomed to the attitude of reverence for Roman law which has been sanctified by centuries of tradition in the western world, the modern reader might be inclined to take Dio at his word. On the other hand, platitudes of this kind were common enough under the Pax Romana, and some feeling of suspicion might be aroused by the fact that the jurists themselves were not certain whether the law was an art or a science. It is prudent to reflect that Dio was not, of course, referring to the *Corpus Juris Civilis* of Justinian, that imposing monument to a thousand years of legal evolution from which the popular concept of Roman law is now derived. Roman law had quite a different aspect in the second century A.D. Even Justinian's great *Corpus* is marred by serious imperfections: some of these stem from the haste in which the compilation was made, and others from an apparent disregard for the virtues of logical arrangement. Nevertheless, the law of the sixth century is flawless when compared with that of Dio's day. By the same token, there had been changes in the two centuries that separated Dio from Cicero even though this earlier period did not achieve the same even progress as that realized between Hadrian and Justinian.

Cicero, that "Eternal Lawyer," is just as symbolic of the history of Roman law as the redoubtable lawgiver, Justinian, but the two would not have seen eye to eye on legal matters. The slipshod legal free-for-all of the Ciceronian Age would have infuriated Justinian, just as Cicero would have been offended by the autocratic restrictions imposed upon the profession in the later period; Cicero might even have lacked the patience to complete the five-year law curriculum established by Justinian's legislation. Neither Cicero nor Justinian would have been satisfied with the legal climate of the year 100 A.D. Justinian might have approved of the growing judicial authority of the emperor, but he would have found little else to his liking. Cicero would have been shocked by the growth of imperial power, and he would have scoffed at the scholarly jurists. Although disheartened by the lack of spectacular cases in which to employ his talents, he might have been somewhat consoled by the acclaim that was given to the courtroom orator and by the comfortable assurance that the old drudgery of legal apprenticeship was no longer thought essential.

Many of the profound changes in Roman law that occurred in the half-millennium separating Cicero and Justinian were made after the establishment of the autocracy by Diocletian and Constantine, but the first major alterations in the judicial system began under Hadrian in the second century A.D. Hadrian's wisdom as an administrator and the advisability of the changes which he introduced are by no means obscured by a survey of legal affairs as revealed in the writings of Tacitus, Pliny the Younger, and Quintilian, authors who flourished in the preceding generation.

Even in the days of Cicero, the legal profession had shown a tendency to divide itself into two groups of specialists: those who studied the law, and those who appeared in the courts as trial lawyers. The first group, the *juris prudentes*, were the product of an evolution that had begun in the third century B.C. The prudentes were learned men, experts in civil law, whose advice came to be sought by magistrates and private individuals. They gave "responses" to legal questions, advised on matters of procedure, and drafted legal forms. Important cogs in the judicial machinery of the first century B.C., the prudentes did not receive compensation for their services nor did they often practice law in any formal way; they were content to write on legal subjects and to perform their consultative functions, but occasionally they were teachers of a sort: Cicero, for example, studied law under Quintus Mucius Scaevola and thoroughly detested the hard work and meticulous attention to detail required by this apprenticeship.

The second group of specialists, the trial lawyers or advocates, rose to prominence after the establishment of the *quaestiones*, the jury courts, which originated in the second century B.C. First devised to try cases of extortion involving provincial governors, the *quaestiones* were later assigned jurisdiction over other criminal suits concerned with sacrilege and peculation, murder, treason, corrupt election practices, forgery of wills, violence, kidnapping, and the like. The primarily political aspects of many of the cases coming before these courts attracted much attention and provided an opportunity for the contesting advocates to secure political advancement; Cicero's victory in the trial of Verres, for example, assured his success in the arena of politics. Before a jury, and particularly in these special kinds of cases, persuasion and fine oratory were all-important; a profound knowledge of the law was seldom essential to winning a case. The spectacular nature of these trials and the substantial rewards for forensic success had an irresistible attraction for ambitious extroverts like Cicero. At the same time, the study of the law itself seemed less and less important and certainly uninteresting.

The advocates of the early principate were the professional descendants of Cicero, but they inherited all of his worst traits in an exaggerated form and none of his good ones. Oratory was supreme; legal knowledge counted for nothing. Many of the most famous and active trial lawyers were solely operators with only a perfunctory knowledge of the law. Specialization had proceeded to a point where the opening speech might be delivered by some famous pleader who had not studied the case at all; after an impassioned address, he would leave the courtroom, and the rest of the trial would be handled by lesser lights who were more familiar with the issues at stake.[2] The attitude of Pliny the Younger seems to have been typical of these latter-day advocates. When he praised a rising young lawyer, it was for his oratorical ability and not for his legal knowledge. Pliny himself often polished up his courtroom speeches for publication; sometimes he could be induced to repeat his court performance privately for a group of friends although he hesitated to do this when the speech involved any legal subtleties since these would be uninteresting to his audience.

In the *Dialogus* of Tacitus one of the participants says that an advocate can win a great reputation for himself and may raise himself from a humble position to one of great power. This was true in a hollow sort of way. A successful advocate enjoyed great prestige, but it did not have the same meaning as in Cicero's day. There were no longer any great cases on which the fate of the government might depend. Many of the old crimes, says the speaker, were still being committed, but the trials of important persons would take place in the senate, instead of before the *quaestiones,* and often under the presidency of the emperor. Rather slyly people said that crimes were less frequent in the modern well-regulated state than in republican times; they added that it was one thing to instruct and convince the people and another to argue before a ruler who was wisdom incarnate. The fact was that in many of the treason trials of the Julio-Claudian and Flavian periods even the most spirited and skillful defense could not have saved people whom the emperor wished to destroy. This made a mockery of justice, but, even in better times, the independence of the judiciary suffered from the right of the emperor to hear appeals; there were numerous instances in which the ruler saw fit to temper sentences that were deservedly severe.

Made wary by their experiences in the first century of the empire and especially during the reign of Domitian, the advocates who appeared before the senate under Nerva and Trajan were not sure that the new and much-advertised *libertas* was a reality. The younger Pliny had been heard to say that there were certain cases which an advocate was bound to undertake: cases involving one's friends or persons in need, cases which tended to set a precedent, and those of a splendid and illustrious kind in which the senate might ask a man to participate. About the year 100 A.D., however, when the senate asked Pliny to prosecute Priscus, the ex-governor of Africa, he begged off on the pretext that he was too busy in his new treasury post. Nervous and worried by a renewal of the senate's request, Pliny sounded out the emperor. When Trajan assured him that it was the duty of a good citizen to comply with the wishes of the senate, Pliny allowed his fame to overtake him since it was clear that the princeps wished the prosecution to go forward.

Both Pliny and Tacitus appeared as advocates for the government's case against Priscus. It was no secret that the man was guilty of extortion; he had already asked for the appointment of a special commission to settle the amount in damages due to the province of Africa. By this maneuver Priscus had hoped to avoid an actual trial, but then it was disclosed that he was also open to a charge of bribery. Despite a five-hour speech by Pliny, the trial was completed in about three days. Priscus was convicted, and Pliny and Tacitus received the thanks of a grateful senate.

Shortly after this triumph, Pliny was again in demand as a prosecutor. This time, Classicus, the governor of Baetica, was being sued by the whole province. Pliny found the case more attractive than the prosecution of Priscus since the defendant had recently confessed his guilt by committing suicide; this certainly diminished the possibility of any personal recriminations, and it would make it easier to convict the governor's subordinates who were co-defendants in the affair. Once again our hero was victorious.

These two trials of provincial governors which occurred almost simultaneously had more in common than the fact that Pliny acted as prosecutor in both cases. It was not significant that Priscus came from Baetica and Classicus from Africa — the Baeticans sardonically remarked that they had been paid in their own coin — but it was probably not a coincidence that both governors had been appointed by Nerva. One might suspect that the senility of the aged princeps had been an invitation to corruption. On the other hand, the trials might have been the result of political infighting encouraged by the death of Nerva and the accession of Trajan. Some importance may be attached to the fact that Salvius Liberalis, who had been suffect consul in the same year as Priscus, acted for the defense in both cases.

Most of Pliny's pleading seems to have been done in civil suits involving wills and inheritances before the centumviral court. The one hundred and eighty jurors comprising this court were divided into four panels which might meet separately under the *decemviri stlitibus judicandis* or be combined under a praetor for an important case. It was the fashion to sneer a bit about the unimportance of the *centumviri* before whom fledgling advocates might try their wings, first making sure to bring along friends and even hired claquers to applaud their efforts. Nevertheless, Pliny recalled with pride the packed houses before which he performed, the crowds so dense that he could scarcely reach his place on the floor and the galleries loaded with people who leaned perilously over the railings to see and hear the action. He did not forget to mention the young man of noble birth who lost his tunic in the press and stood in nothing but his toga as he listened to Pliny declaim for seven hours.

These civil contests were frequently spirited; sometimes the advocates became most uncivil, and no holds were barred. Suetonius gives us the Latin version of the "Have you stopped beating your wife?" approach in his story about the advocate who challenged a man to swear by the bodies of his unburied father and mother.[3] Pliny's *bête noire* was a clever and unscrupulous lawyer named Regulus who had once put him in a tight spot. During the reign of Domitian, they had been opponents in a suit before the *centumviri*. Pliny incautiously cited an opinion that had been given by a jurist who had recently been exiled by the emperor. Regulus was on Pliny like a tiger asking for his opinion of Modestus, the jurist in question, but Pliny managed to wriggle out of the predicament by saying that it was improper to answer a question concerning a convicted person. He never forgave Regulus and often referred to him in the most uncomplimentary terms as a legacy hunter, the Latin for ambulance chaser. This "bad man unskilled in the art of speaking" may have been as evil as Pliny claimed, but he was apparently a little too much for Pliny to handle. A showman who wore a patch over his left or right eye depending on whether he was acting for the plaintiff or the defendant, Regulus always drew a good crowd for each performance; after Regulus died, Pliny confessed that he missed him because the courts would never be the same without this lively charlatan.

Pliny had studied under Quintilian, but he seems not to have listened attentively to Quintilian's advice about the advocate's profession. A large portion of the *Institutes* was devoted to the problems of preparing and presenting a case for trial. Quintilian was a practicing advocate as well as a teacher, and he was proud of his courtroom triumphs. Although he did not, of course, minimize the importance of oratory, he did insist on a knowledge of the law and a careful study of the strategy for each case. Because of their ignorance of the law, said Quintilian, the advocates were becoming mere messengers dependent upon the advice of others. Attention to details was important. One must study the documents relating to the case, question one's client again and again, subject him to a pretrial cross-examination, and remember that it is better to know what is superfluous than to be ignorant of what is essential, for it could be embarrassing to have to get the facts in court from the opposition. In possession of all the information, the advocate must then try to divine how the opposition would conduct its case; he must also attempt to put himself in the place of the judge, and it was always helpful to know something of the character of the judge himself.

In the actual trial, it would inevitably be easier to conduct the prosecution than the defense. The prosecutor could mass his facts, while the lawyer for the defense would be better advised to divide them. One must always be alert and not committed to one line of procedure only. It was all right to fib a little, but "a liar should have a good memory." The judge should be handled carefully; it was not a good idea to suggest that he might have been bribed or to act as if you mistrusted his memory or understanding of what had already been said. In the peroration there could be an appeal to equity, and an emotional display might be more effective than logic; one might supplicate the judge with moderation, but this should never be overdone because "nothing dries quicker than tears."

By the reign of Trajan the heyday of the forensic orator was drawing to a close. For two centuries the advocates had monopolized the limelight, but now it was the turn of the scholarly jurists. Right from the beginning of the principate, the emperors had needed to seek competent legal advice because many circumstances combined to promote a steady growth in the judicial functions of the princeps. Such advice could not be had from the advocates who were becoming less and less knowledgeable in the law. Therefore the emperors turned to the prudentes who were employed not only as advisers to the ruler himself but also to the magistrates who had judicial responsibilities. In addition, there was a growing tendency to employ the jurists as judges for the very cases in which the advocates often appeared.[4]

The battle lines were soon drawn, for the jurists and the forensic orators were mutually contemptuous. We begin to hear complaints from the orators that the judges are unsympathetic. It is said that judges are more interested in concluding than deciding cases; that the judge travels faster than counsel; that judges limit speakers and call them back from digressions; that a judge is anxious to come to the strongest point, and, if he is busy or important or rude, he will insist that the orator state his case without delay. This was unbearable. Everyone knew that jurists were dullards and even boors. They were the misfits who lacked the talent to become advocates. Pliny told with delight a story about a jurist named Javolenus who broke up a poetry session by vociferously emerging from scholarly meditation when he thought the poet had spoken his name. There had been some doubt regarding the sanity of Javolenus, and this confirmed everyone's suspicions. The mad Javolenus, strange to relate, had already served in various official capacities in Dalmatia, Numidia, Britain, Germany, and Syria, and he was to become a member of the imperial consilium under

Trajan and Hadrian; he was also the teacher of the great jurist Salvius Julianus.

Licinius Nepos, praetor in 105 A.D., may not have been a jurist, but he certainly acted like one. He started out by fining jurors, even those of senatorial rank, when they failed to turn up for sessions of his court. Then he discovered a bashful advocate named Tuscilius Nominatus who had been paid a fee of over 2000 denarii to represent the Vicentini and had then failed to make an appearance in court. Nepos not only secured the disbarment of Nominatus but also dug up a decree of the senate which forbade fees for advocates. The other praetors scarcely knew what to make of a man who bothered to read the statutes and decrees of the senate; the presiding magistrate of the *centumviri* recessed his court until he could decide what to do. Officially, the acceptance of fees had always been frowned upon although the emperors had occasionally yielded to pressure from the advocates so far as to set certain maximum amounts for fees; unfortunately, this was like raising the ceiling on the national debt in our felicitous age because one good boost always seemed to deserve another. Pliny paraded his own virtue with great ostentation, proclaiming that he had never charged for his services, but his splendour was quite solitary. Others were accustomed to accept and even to stipulate fees. Quintilian condemned bargaining for a fee or making it proportionate to the stature of the cause although he thought nevertheless that remuneration was right and proper.

Nepos finally overreached himself and got into a hassle with a real jurist, Juventius Celsus, over a matter of procedure in the senate. The battle was hot and the contestants abusive. Celsus was never one to be over-polite; he always called a spade a spade, and he was accustomed to say quite directly that people who disagreed with him, even the other jurists, were stupid. Although Pliny was present at the altercation between Nepos and Celsus, he was not interested in following the argument; instead, he criticized the speakers for using notes — a good orator could have spoken extemporaneously.

Pliny was in seventh heaven *(maximam cepi voluptatem)* when he was invited to Centumcellae to participate for a few days as a member of the imperial consilium or council. In a letter he described the case which the emperor tried in the presence of the consilium — a noted citizen of Ephesus was acquitted of a charge of treason, an army wife was sentenced for adultery, and there was a case involving the alleged forging of a will. The emperor listened to the pleading, consulted his advisors, and rendered his decisions.

This rather informal and old-fashioned manner of doing business was soon to be changed, for Hadrian established a new kind of onsilium with permanent salaried members many of whom were ading jurists.[5] Such experts were not new to the consilia of the rincipate, but their numbers in proportion to the other members seem o have been increasing; Pliny may have sensed that the jurists were aining a position more influential than that of an occasional guest erformer like himself. With the exception of Titius Aristo, whom he dmired, Pliny did not care much for jurists. Aristo was a member of 'rajan's consilium, but Pliny had no good words for Celsus or Javolenus 'riscus who not only served Trajan but Hadrian as well; neither did liny mention Neratius Priscus who duplicated their long service and, it vas said, was also considered to be of imperial calibre.[6]

From the time of Hadrian the legal experts who advised judges and nagistrates were likewise given salaried posts. These jurists, who had he title of adsessores, comites, or consilarii, were attached to the onsilia of consuls, praetors, city prefects, provincial governors, and raetorian prefects. The adsessores became permanent secretaries who ctually did much of the work which came under the province of the nagistrates whom they served.[7]

The princeps was more than a chief magistrate who needed advice to ulfill his judicial functions; he was also a source of law. "An imperial onstitution," says Gaius, "is what the emperor ordains by a *decretum,* n edict, or a letter."[8] The first was a decision handed down by the mperor when he tried a case before the consilium in the manner escribed by Pliny. An edict was an imperial proclamation; the antonine Constitution of 212 A.D. or Diocletian's Edict of Prices are vell-known examples of this type. An epistula might be a simple letter ke one of Trajan's replies to Pliny during the latter's Bithynian overnorship. This was also known as a rescript, although the term escript was similarly applied to subscriptiones, the replies of an mperor to petitions. Beginning with Hadrian, the emperor might be sked for a decision on a point of law involved in some specific case. 'he emperor's rescript in this instance would thus resemble the esponse of a jurist.

Under the early empire the jurisconsults had continued to give esponses as in republican times, but there were bound to be changes in he system. Augustus had bestowed upon certain jurists the privilege of iving responses on the authority of the princeps although this did not nfringe upon the right of other jurists to be consulted nor did it mean hat a magistrate or judge must accept the opinion given under the uthority granted by the emperor. It is possible that Hadrian may have iven some added prestige to his imperial jurisconsults; it was inevitable n any case that their responses should carry more weight than those of

an ordinary jurist. On the other hand, the codification of the praetor's
edict during Hadrian's reign would tend to diminish the importance of
and even the necessity for responses relating to many phases of the civil
law.[9]

Nevertheless, as the old order changed, the jurists gained rather than
lost in the process. They became official rather than unofficial cogs in
the judicial machinery of the empire. In addition, the growth of formal
legal training made them better and better prepared for the duties
which they were called upon to perform.

As early as the first century A.D., Seneca had remarked that, while
the study of poetry and history was relaxing, the training in law and
mathematics must be classed as severe. By his day there were two rival
law schools in Rome known as the Sabinians and the Proculians.[10] The
Sabinian school had been founded by a jurist named Cassius who
flourished during the reign of Nero, while the Proculians traced their
origin from the teaching of Antistius Labeo, a contemporary of
Augustus. It is believed that both schools were actual establishments
complete with regular teachers who alternated their lectures with
practice by the students in disputation. Nerva, Celsus, and Neratius
Priscus were Proculians, while Javolenus, Salvius Julianus, and Gaius
were Sabinians. The rivalry between the two schools was very bitter
but it is hard to ascertain in what way they differed from each other
except that the Proculians may have been Peripatetics and the
Sabinians, Stoics. Unfortunately, it is not possible to follow the
development of the schools of law in the period between Hadrian and
the autocracy. Even the quarrels of the Sabinians and the Proculians
cease to be mentioned. Instead, we are left to draw inferences about the
educational system from the writings of the great jurists who held the
stage from Hadrian to Severus Alexander; the proof of the pudding is in
their work.

A major reform of Hadrian and one that greatly affected the work
of the jurists was the codification of the praetor's edict. Under the
republic it had become customary for each magistrate upon beginning
his year of office to issue an edict or proclamation which set forth the
principles by which the office in question would be administered. In
the case of those officials concerned with the administration of justice
particularly the praetors and provincial governors, the edict would state
the maxims of law and forms of procedure to be followed. Slanted in
the direction of increasing equity, the praetor's edict had led to the
formulation of new legal principles and new remedies at law. In theory
each official issued a new edict, but in practice he would employ many
precedents established by his predecessors, and the growth of the edict

would be by accretion rather than by abrupt new departures from tradition. The city praetor was chiefly responsible for the development of the civil law, which applied only to Romans, but the praetor peregrinus and the provincial governors, who dealt with both Romans and foreigners, had to take into account existing laws and customs which were non-Roman in origin and firmly established, and there can be little doubt that their edicts underwent a more rapid evolution than that of the city praetor. It is also quite evident that the magistrates who issued the edicts would not ordinarily be well versed in the law and must have relied heavily upon advice from the jurisconsults.

In the early principate the edict seems to have become pretty well stabilized; thus, Hadrian's order which directed Salvius Julianus to codify the praetorian and aedilician edicts was a logical procedure. Henceforth the edict could not be altered by the praetors or aediles; future modifications would take the form of imperial constitutions drafted by the jurists of the emperor's consilium. Codification was a process characteristic of the age, for in many fields people were compiling and systematizing knowledge. Salvius Julianus, Pliny the Elder, Vitruvius, Frontinus, and Athenaeus had much in common. At the same time, the codification of the edict was a piece of systematization which a growing bureaucracy made necessary.

The content and the arrangement of the praetorian edict can be reconstructed with some degree of confidence. It dealt with procedures, remedies, formulae, and the execution of justice. The later commentators sometimes quote from the document. These quotations are often introduced by the phrase "the praetor says." Among the examples might be cited, "Where a man is alleged to have harboured a slave of either sex belonging to another or induced him or her maliciously to act in any way with intent to deteriorate his or her character, I will allow an action against him for twice what the matter comes to," or "where an act is done through fear I will not uphold it," or "if they have no advocate, I will give them one," etc.[11]

Far from suffering from the limitation on the "private" *ius respondendi* imposed by Hadrian and by the changes in function which the codification of the edict introduced, the jurists found that the exchange of private for official station widened the field of their activities and gave them a new prestige. In the service of the emperor, a series of great jurists now served at the court, and a new age dawned that was an important one in Roman legal history. In their official capacity they were assisting the most powerful of all magistrates, the emperor. The jurists were able to exert a tremendous influence upon the law by suggesting imperial legislation and also by clarifying these new laws through subsequent interpretations, but at the same time they were expounding and systematizing the whole of Roman law by studies and monographs that lay in a scholarly field quite outside that of their official duties since they were engaged in writing commentaries on the law and also in reviewing, criticizing, and emending the commentaries of one another. This was an era of academic, scholarly disputation in which the practical and the theoretical were mingled. In other words the legal studies of this age were really a part of, or were affected by the prevailing intellectual climate of the second and early third centuries. One has only to follow the squabbles of the grammarians or compare the *Institutes* of Gaius with those of Quintilian to see that the rhetoricians, orators, philosophers, and lawyers of this age were very much alike in their attitudes and activities. This is not surprising since they were the products of a common system of basic education.

On the other hand, the essentially non-Roman origin of some of the great jurists suggests that they did not get their major training at Rome. Julianus came from Africa where there was a law school at Carthage in later times; Gaius seems to have had his origin somewhere in the Roman East, while Papinian was a Syrian and may have been trained at Beyrut. Ulpian came from Tyre. Provincial in origin, these people could hardly have escaped being influenced by provincial law, and it is possible that they may have introduced the first elements of contamination or vulgarization into Roman law and thus encouraged a trend that became so obvious under the autocracy.

It was probably not a coincidence that the greatest age of the legal commentators began with and followed upon the codification of the edict. The codification was not only the first of its kind among the Romans, but it also gave the future commentators something to get their teeth into. Before a century had passed Gaius, Pomponius, Paul and Ulpian had written commentaries on the edict. Other commentaries were written by the jurists on the laws (leges) and on the decrees of the senate; then there were commentaries on commentaries, extracts from the legal literature, "problematic works" containing questions and answers relating to specific legal problems, collections of legal maxims and abstract statements of law. Last of all, there were textbooks of which the *Institutes* of Gaius provides the principal surviving example.[12] It is not known whether Gaius actually wrote the *Institutes* or whether some pupil published his lecture notes, but the first edition appears to date from about 161 A.D. The work is divided into four books, the first of which is concerned with the Law of Persons, the second and third with the Law of Things, and the fourth with the Law of Actions. The *Institutes* was influential for centuries; it was used by

Justinian's compilers as the principal source for their official textbook
which they produced for law students in the sixth century.

A good example of the activities of the jurists is provided by the
following extract from Justinian's *Digest* which quotes from Ulpian on
negotia gesta (voluntary action): [13]

> Does the law go so far as to bestow on me a right of action for
> the expense I have occurred (acting in behalf of someone else)? I
> should say I have a good right of action.... Accordingly if a man
> repaired a house or cured a sick slave, he will have a good action
> on *negotia gesta,* even if the house is now burnt or the slave is
> dead: this Labeo approves of. However, according to Celsus,
> Proculus says in a note on the passage in Labeo that the action
> need not always be allowed.... Take the case, for instance, of a
> man repairing a house which the owner had abandoned because
> he could not afford the expense of it.... In such a case, says
> Proculus, he is laying a burden on the owner, if we adopt
> Labeo's view, since everybody is at liberty to abandon his
> property.... This opinion of Proculus is neatly upheld to ridicule
> by Celsus. A man, he says, to have an action on *negotia gesta*
> must have managed the affair beneficially.... Similar to the above
> rule is one we meet with in Julianus ....

Or again:

> ....according to Aristo's well expressed reply to Celsus, there is
> an obligation formed.... Accordingly, I should say that Julianus
> was rightly taken to task by Mauricianus in reference to the
> following case, etc.

And so it went until the establishment of the autocracy by
Diocletian and Constantine. By the fourth century judicial disputation
was discouraged and even forbidden. The free-for-all of the second
century was outlawed by the autocracy because a mere subject could
not be allowed to contradict the emperor. As a matter of fact, much of
the modification of the praetor's edict and the clarification of the laws
had been accomplished by imperial rescript with increasing frequency
from the second century onward. It is significant that the earliest
rescripts in Justinian's code come from the reign of Hadrian, the
emperor who had done so many other things to alter the legal
organization of the empire. Again and again an emperor is seen to
intervene and humanize the law: [14]

If you have clearly ascertained that Aelius Priscus was in such a state of insanity that he was permanently out of his mind.... and no suspicion is left that he was simulating insanity when he killed his mother, you need not concern yourself with the question of how he should be punished since his insanity is punishment enough.... (Marcus Aurelius and Commodus)

Or again:

When Marcianus said, "I used no violence," the emperor replied, "Do you think there is no violence except where people are wounded? It is just as much a case of violence wherever it happens that a man who thinks he has a right to something demands to have it given up without going to the court. If anyone is shown to me to be in possession of or to have taken anything belonging to his debtor.... to have laid down the law for himself in the matter, he shall forfeit the right of a creditor." (Marcus Aurelius)

Industrious and indefatigable though they were, the jurists of the Pax Romana had their faults.[15] They never approached their subject from a historical point of view, and this was to prevent them from making a methodical arrangement of their material as it accumulated into an unmanageable mass. There was never any attempt to achieve a thoroughly logical order of the subject matter even in the *Digest* of Justinian or the *Code*. Legal philosophy was another topic which had no appeal for the jurists; in this area the advocates made a better showing than their learned contemporaries. The formulation of abstract principles was also distrusted by the jurists; Javolenus was reputed to have said that abstract formulations in private law were generally fallacious. The chief interest was in case law, yet citations were rare and the jurist himself was presumed to possess sufficient authority to pronounce an opinion rather than relying upon an earlier decision or arguing out the case in a logical manner. There was a pedantry and lack of imagination in the thinking of the jurists that had its parallel in the scholarship of their age.

Roman law was characterized by some curious procedures and situations. In earlier times suits were based on statute law which allowed certain definite legal actions. A plaintiff might approach the defendant and say, "I affirm that you owe me so many sesterces; I ask whether you affirm or deny this." If the defendant denied the debt, the plaintiff said, "Since you deny, I give you notice to appear on such and such a day in order to take a *iudex* (judge)." By the imperial period, this sort of procedure had pretty well disappeared except for cases tried by the centumviral court, especially cases involving inheritance. Instead, the so-called formulary procedure was now common. In this kind of action the defendant would be notified of the nature of the claim and summoned to appear before the praetor. On the appointed day, the formula or charge would be laid before the praetor who would be asked to grant the action and appoint a *iudex,* or judge, to try the case on the basis of the formula. The type of action and the formula employed would have to be drawn from the praetor's edict. The formula itself had several parts. In its simplest form, it would have an *intentio,* the statement of the claim, and a *condemnatio* which empowered the *iudex* to condemn or absolve the defendant. In the pattern formulae the plaintiff was called Aulus Agerius (from *agit,* he who brings the action), and the defendant, Numerius Negidius (from *numerat,* he who pays, and *negat,* denies). This provides a vague and not exact parallel to our John Doe and Richard Roe. A simple formula might run: "If it appears that N.N. ought to pay 10,000 sesterces to A.A., the judge is to condemn N.N. to pay A.A. 10,000 sesterces; if it does not appear, he is to absolve." If the plaintiff made an over-claim – if he claimed 10,000 where only 9,000 was due – the *iudex* was bound to dismiss the suit. If there was an underclaim, the plaintiff would get only what he claimed in the suit and could not sue for the balance until a new praetor came into office. This all seems rather clumsy, but the formulary procedure represented a great advance over the earlier *legis actiones* which allowed no leeway whatever. For example, under the *legis actiones,* if a man was bringing suit over a vineyard and claimed damage to "vines" instead of "trees" – the wording used in the law – his suit would be thrown out.

The *Digest* of Justinian hints at all kinds of curious cases known to the courts of the republic and early empire. If, for example, a man tending a shop was not empowered to enter into contracts, a notice must be posted publicly to that effect. "Publicly set up is understood as meaning, in plain letters, so that the notice can easily be read from the ground, that is, in the front of the shop or place where the business is carried on, not in an obscure place, but in the open. May it be in Greek, or must it be in Latin? I think this is according to the character of the place."[16]

There was much about injuries:[17]

The father will get an amount equivalent to his loss of profit from his son's services occasioned by the destruction of his son's eye, besides the cost of medical expense. If a surgeon operates unskillfully, an action is allowed, or if he make the wrong use of a drug, or if an operation is successful but further treatment is omitted.

A man hires a slave to lead a mule and puts the animal under his charge; the slave thereupon ties the line by which he is holding the mule to his thumb, and the mule breaks away, tears the slave's thumb off, and then throws itself over a height.... an action can be brought against the owner of the slave.

Two slaves try to leap over a heap of burning straw, they come into collision, both fall, and one of the two is burnt to death; here no action can be brought as long as it is not ascertained which of the two was upset by the other.

It can be assumed that the Rhodian Sea Law which was used in the Byzantine period was equally valid in the Roman period. Under this code, a certain amount of space was allotted to each passenger on board ship. A man must have a space at least five feet in length and a foot and a half wide; a woman needed an area only twenty inches square, while half that would suffice for a child. Passengers could neither split wood nor fry fish while aboard, and they must deposit their gold with the captain for safekeeping. In case of shipwreck, the passenger who managed to save some of his belongings must contribute something to make up for the loss of the ship. Mariners frequently stole one another's anchors, and sailors were always fighting despite a law which recommended that they dispute with words only. A sailor who signed on for a cruise was regarded as a slave who must execute all commands. In heavy seas the captain was responsible for water damage to his cargo; silk, linen, or grain must be provided with a protective covering.[18]

The Roman law relating to servitudes took into account a number of interesting situations in which people did or did not have the right of use or access to the property of others. This also involved water rights and what we would call a building code as well as other related matters:[19]

When a man is carried on a chair or litter [across the property of someone else], he is said to have an *iter* .... if he has an *actus* he can take a wagon or drive draft animals. But in neither case has he a right to drag stones or timber; and some say he cannot carry a spear in an upright position, as he would not do by way of driving or walking, moreover fruit might be injured by it.

People were not supposed to build their homes in such a way as to obstruct the view of their neighbors. The height of the structures was limited in such cases, and no one could prevent his neighbor from getting a view of a garden or a park or waterfront, but it was decided that, if a man complained that his view of a statue was obstructed, he must prove that he knew something about the historical or religious meaning of the masterpiece he wanted so desperately to see. In Byzantine law, and possibly in Roman law, street cafes were prohibited, and no one could tether a horse in front of his house. It was a crowning mercy that fish curing establishments and cheese factories were banished to a reasonable distance from the city limits.

Gambling was frowned upon, except where the wagering was done on an athletic contest in which the performers were competing to win some distinction. The owners of slaves or fathers of minors could recover the gambling losses of their charges. Dicing could be punished by a fine or sentence to hard labor especially in cases where people forced others to play "sometimes so doing from the very first, and sometimes compelling the winner to continue playing when they themselves had lost."

Injuries caused the jurists some difficulty in determining the proper course of action for redress. Injuries inflicted by animals posed a problem because it was necessary to decide whether the animal had been behaving with a natural ferocity or whether the damage had been caused by negligence. An inexperienced muledriver might be responsible for injuries caused by his runaway animals, just as a weak driver might face a charge of negligence "because no man ought to undertake a task in which he knows that his want of strength will be a source of peril to others."

Nothing can cap, however, the situation posed in *Digest* IX. ii. 11:

If several persons are playing at ball, one of whom gives the ball a rather hard stroke and so drives it against the hand of a barber, and thereby a slave whom the barber has in his hands has his throat cut, in consequence of the razor being knocked against it, whichever party was guilty of negligence is liable.... Proculus says the negligence is the barber's; and certainly, if he was carrying on his trade in a spot where the sport above mentioned is usually practised.... he is to some extent accountable, though, on the other hand, there is some sense to the remark that where a man puts himself in the hands of a barber who has set up his stool in a dangerous place, he has only himself to blame.

Roman law, like Rome itself, was not built in a day. From the epoch of the Twelve Tables to the time of Cicero, certain improvements were made with the substitution of the formulary procedure for the *legis actiones* and the development of the praetor's edict and the *quaestiones*. By the second century, when the reforms of Hadrian were beginning to take effect, and the bureaucracy was commencing to diminish the individualism of the legal experts, the law was on the road toward its final stage of relative perfection. It was to take, however, two hundred and fifty years of autocracy from Diocletian to Constantine to produce what the world calls Roman law, a law which by the sixth century, sad to relate, is more Byzantine than Roman.

FOOTNOTES

1. Suetonius, *On Grammarians*, XXII.

2. Quintilian, *Institutes*, XII, 8.

3. Suetonius, *On Rhetoricians*, VI.

4. F. Schulz, *History of Roman Legal Science*, Oxford 1946, p. 111 ff., especially p. 118.

5. Schulz, *op. cit.*, pp. 117-118.

6. *Scriptores Historiae Augustae, Hadrian*, IV, 8; XVIII, 1. On the jurists see Schulz, *op. cit.*, p. 102 ff.; H. F. Jolowicz, *Historical Introduction to the Study of Roman Law*, Cambridge 1954, p. 391 ff.

7. Schulz, *op. cit.*, p. 117.

8. Gaius, *Institutes*, I, 5.

9. On the *ius respondendi*, see Schulz, *op. cit.*, p. 112 ff.; Jolowicz, *op. cit.*, p. 369 ff.

10. *Digest*, II, 47-53; Schulz, *op. cit.*, pp. 119-123; Jolowicz, *op. cit.*, pp. 388-391.

11. *Digest*, XI, 3, 1; IV, 2, 1.

12. F. de Zulueta, *Institutes of Gaius*, 2 vols., Oxford 1946 provides a convenient edition.

13. *Digest*, III, 5, 9; II, 14, 7 as translated by C. H. Monro.

14. *Ibid.*, I, 18, 14; IV, 2, 13.

15. Schulz, *op. cit.*, p. 124 ff.

16. *Digest*, XIV, 3, 11.

17. *Ibid.*, IX, 2, 7-8; 2, 27; 2, 45.

18. On the Rhodian Sea Law, see W. Ashburner, *Rhodian Sea Law*, Oxford 1909.

19. *Digest*, VIII, 3, 7.

Pox Romana

*Phidon did not purge me or even touch me, but having a fever I
remembered his name and died.*

Greek Anthology

*A physician is the only person that can kill another with
impunity.*

Pliny the Elder

ABOUT SUNSET ONE EVENING during the reign of Marcus
Aurelius the Greek physician Galen was called to the palace for an
urgent consultation. The emperor himself was ill, and his personal
physicians believed him to be on the verge of something serious — a
febrile attack, they said. Galen found Marcus with a stomach ache and a
perfectly normal pulse. He quickly diagnosed the trouble as the result
of overeating, recommended the application of wool impregnated with
spikenard ointment, the ancient equivalent of the hot water bottle, and
said that for an ordinary person he would prescribe a dose of wine
sprinkled with pepper. Galen's advice was followed; the emperor even
insisted on taking the plebeian wine and pepper and quickly recovered
what passed for his health.

We cannot be sure in this case whether Galen was relying on his long
medical experience or upon his personal knowledge of the patient, for
the philosopher emperor was rarely philosophical about his health. He
was, to put it bluntly, a hypochondriac of long standing. Poor Marcus
could scarcely have been anything else surrounded as he was by a host
of fellow-sufferers who complained continuously as well as exquisitely
about their ailments while he himself followed a strict regimen of pills,
powders, and doses. Before Galen arrived to save the day on this
particular occasion, the emperor had had a dose of bitter aloes and his
usual theriac and wine. Theriac was not a tonic, as Cassius Dio later
supposed; it was a concoction administered every day in small
quantities to render the emperor immune to poison. Old Mithridates of
Pontus had taken theriac for years with the disturbing consequence that
he could not even poison himself when he wished to commit suicide
after his defeat by Pompey. The theriac used by Marcus Aurelius
possessed an even greater inconvenience: one of its ingredients was

poppy juice which made the emperor sleepy, but, when the juice was omitted, he suffered from insomnia.

Although Book I of the *Meditations* displays a certain reticence on the subject, one of the influential men in the life of Marcus Aurelius was his African tutor, mentor, and somewhat elder friend, Marcus Cornelius Fronto. The extant correspondence between Marcus Aurelius and Fronto is voluminous and revealing.[1] It gives the distinct impression that Fronto was well pleased with Marcus as his student in oratory despite the fact that Marcus later deserted oratory for philosophy. We may even suspect that the pupil surpassed the master as an orator, but, although he tried hard and protested loudly and often, Marcus could never outdo Fronto in frailty of health.

Early in the correspondence as it is now arranged, Fronto complains of insomnia, then a pain in his elbow, then his gout. While Fronto is confined to his bed, Marcus Aurelius catches a cold from walking about in his slippers. This develops into a sore throat which is relieved by swallowing some honey water and then ejecting it again; Marcus refuses to say that he gargled the honey water because the use of the word *gargarisso* might expose him to a charge of having committed a barbarism. Fronto, however, has the last word because he develops a pain in his shoulder, knee, elbow, and ankle. In a later contest of miseries, Fronto leads off with a pain in the neck. Marcus is forced to confess that he himself got through the night and managed to eat breakfast, but "we will see what the night brings" and "you can certainly gauge my feelings when I learned that you had been taken with a pain in the neck." Fronto was generous: with the pain in his neck, he no longer had one in his foot. Marcus continued to improve and was able to take a bath and drink some wine, but then his daughter saved the family honor by getting the flux. As she recovered, Fronto got a pain in his toe which spread to elbow and neck and finally settled in his groin, first on one side and then on the other. Not satisfied with Marcus' sympathy, Fronto says, "Please acquaint the emperor [Antoninus Pius] with my illness." The pious Antoninus, however, had his own troubles: he suffered from migraine although *he* was not given to complaining.[2]

Some time after this Fronto's attendants were carrying him in a sedan chair from the baths and scraped his knee on a hot pipe. On this occasion Marcus was a bit unsympathetic because Faustina Senior was ill and Faustina Junior was about to have another child. Fronto continued to have pains in his knee, pains in the foot, the flux, etc., etc. His gout was certainly real enough, but it was a fairly common ailment in this period; the ancients ascribed the gout to high living, but modern belief is that it was caused by lead poisoning from the water pipes then in use.

All these little skirmishes, however, were outdone by one series of episodes in which Marcus, for once, came out the victor. Fronto complained of a pain in his knee but confessed having heard that Faustina Junior was ailing. As she deteriorated, Fronto got a bad cold which gave Marcus Aurelius acute pain and burning fever just to think about it. Things went from bad to worse. The climax is described in a letter from Marcus to Fronto:[3]

> My sister was seized with such pain in the privy parts that it was dreadful to see her. Moreover, my mother, in the flurry of the moment, inadvertently ran her side against the corner of the wall, causing us as well as herself great pain by the accident. For myself, when I went to lie down I came upon a scorpion in my bed; however, I was in time to kill it before lying down upon it.

After all this, it is not surprising to learn that Aesculapius was especially worshipped by Antoninus Pius and Marcus Aurelius. Moreover, Fronto and Marcus and their ailing relatives had plenty of company in their misery. Appian, the historian, complains of a gastric disorder; Dio of Prusa laments his feeble health in the thirty-ninth, forty-fifth, forty-eighth, and fifty-second discourses; Pliny refers to illness in his household on many occasions. Plutarch must have been fully conscious of the temper or distemper of his age; putting his shoulder to the wheel, he wrote a dialogue entitled "Rules for the Preservation of Health."

This was a period in which people seemed to be "skeered of livin' and feerd of dyin'." The first might be illustrated by Marcus Aurelius' letters to Fronto and the second by his *Meditations*. On the other hand, real and serious and seemingly incurable illnesses were widespread and even very common before the advent of the series of plagues that began with the reign of Marcus Aurelius and raged throughout the third century. The average life expectancy was not more than thirty-five years. People died young; inscriptions and literary sources show that infant mortality was excessively high; illness and accident took the lives of children and adolescents; the Grim Reaper often cut down the mother along with her new-born child. There were few like Callicratia, the mother of twenty-nine children all of whom survived her although she lived to the age of a hundred and five. More typical were the two brothers who were born and died the same day; or little Corax, aged two; or little Callimachus, aged five, who had "but a small share of life and life's evils." The twin brother of Commodus died at an early age; a child of Herodes died shortly after birth; one of Quintilian's sons did not live more than five years while the other died at ten; Quintilian's wife was buried at nineteen after giving birth to the second son.

Yet this was the Age of Galen, the greatest physician of classical antiquity! By the second century A.D. Rome was crowded with doctors and surgeons; a high degree of specialization had developed; there were public and private hospitals and even state- and city-employed doctors in many towns besides Rome. Medical treatises were being written in abundance, not only by Galen who wrote more than his share, but also by his contemporaries. The doctors seemed very confident of their ability; we know that they often charged exorbitant fees, and many became wealthy through their medical practice. On the other hand, while the doctors often talked about their patients, the latter rarely mentioned their physicians except in the most uncomplimentary terms

The attitude of Pliny the Elder is fairly typical. The medical profession, says Pliny, is monopolized by non-Romans and dominated by Greeks. No one would have confidence in a doctor whose medical vocabulary contained any but Greek terms, but such verbal facility seemed to be about the only qualification for practice. The doctors are unsupervised, free of responsibility, and unscrupulous enough at times to combine fraud, adultery, and poisoning with their healing. Juvenal hints at the casualty rate of the physician Themison, while Martial is violently hostile toward doctors as a whole. The bilious poet of Bilbilis, as he has been called,[4] said one only had to see the doctor Hermocrates in a dream in order to die; of an eye-specialist turned gladiator, he remarked that the man had not changed his methods at all; as for a doctor who had become an undertaker, he could see little alteration either. This last remark has a familiar parallel in the Greek epigram about the cooperation between doctor and sexton. The *Deipnosophistae* agreed that if it were not for the doctors, there would be no one more stupid than the professors.[5] And there is much more of the same

A glance at the medical literature of the first and second centuries A.D. helps to explain the prevailing lack of confidence in the medical profession, for the doctors, like many of their patients, were in a state of flux. In medical theory the influence of the Hippocratic school was still very strong. All the great physicians from the Hellenistic age onward owed more to Hippocrates than they sometimes cared to admit Of course, as time passed the methods of the Father of Medicine had been improved somewhat; furthermore, knowledge of physiology and anatomy had increased. On the other hand, the influence of Greek philosophy had been very strong in medical evolution and not always advantageous. By the Christian era a number of "schools" of medicine had developed.[6] The adherents of one school would feud bitterly with the representatives of rival schools; by and large the best doctors were either the founders of schools or eclectics who had sense enough to pick and choose good elements from a number of systems, but the partisans tended to be dogmatic, bigoted, and ignorant. As Galen said,[7] "Now one person will admire one physician or philosopher, without either having studied their work or practised the logical method so as to be able to separate what are false in their arguments from what are true. The reasons for their admiration are either that their fathers, teachers, or friends were Empirics, Dogmatists, or Methodists, or that So-and-So, belonging to this or that school, was famous in their native town."

The nearest successors to Hippocrates were the Dogmatists who proclaimed medicine a science and depended upon reason and theory. They professed to understand the nature of the body, the origins of disease, and the properties of medicines; starting from reason, they made use of analogy in treating an unfamiliar ailment. The Empiricists, on the other hand, based their practice on experience and experiment. Their medicine was a collection of experience composed of personal observations and the medical records of others. Where a knowledge of anatomy was deemed of prime importance by the Dogmatists, the Empiricists thought it unnecessary. The cause of a disorder was a fundamental concern of the former school, while the latter concentrated on cures. In philosophical descent, the Dogmatists were Peripatetics; the Empiricists, Skeptics.

About the beginning of the first century B.C., a certain Asclepiades began to practice in Rome with great success. Drawing his notions from Epicureanism, Asclepiades taught that all vital functions were based on the movement of atoms; disease resulted when the movement of the atoms of the body was abnormal. Themison, a pupil of Asclepiades, elaborated upon this new kind of theorizing and founded a new school, that of the Methodists. The Methodists believed that if the pores of the body were excessively open or closed as the atoms might be relaxed or constricted, illness would take place; they admitted also a third state of disorder which combined relaxation and construction. These three types of situations represented for the Methodists the triad of possible communities of disease or disease groups. Rejecting the "indications" of the Dogmatists, the Methodists stuck to "appearances." This made things rather simple, so much so, in fact, that the aspiring medical student could learn all he needed to know in six months. Since the Methodists were materialistic and Epicurean, an appropriate reaction set in with the Pneumatists of the first century A.D. who were inspired by Stoic philosophy. They believed that air was drawn from the lungs into the left side of the heart where it was transformed into "natural" and "psychic" pneuma. The first was distributed to the arteries, while the second went to the brain and from thence into the nervous system. The good or bad health of the patient could therefore be judged by feeling the pulse.

In actual medical treatment, of course, more depended upon the experience and skill of the doctor than upon the "school" which he happened to represent. Dogmatists and Empiricists, for example, treated diseases in similar ways, nor was there a great difference in the methods of the Pneumatists, Eclectics, or Methodists who possessed any real talent or skill. It was the dolts and quacks who had to be feared by their patients. In addition, there might be times when professional competition or doctrinal rivalries might stand in the way of competent treatment. The competition at Rome was particularly severe: one physician might do everything in his power to blacken the reputation of another or make ridiculous claims for his own methods; some doctors even solicited the patronage of passers-by. Galen claimed that his successes at Rome aroused such ill feeling among the other physicians that he thought it wise to leave town. On the other hand, Galen himself was militant, argumentative, and often hypercritical; his unpopularity is readily understandable.

There was a strange mixture of sense and nonsense in the medical writers of the Pax Romana. Celsus, Soranus, Rufus, Aretaeus, and Galen all had their virtues and their faults. Celsus, the "Cicero of Medicine," was perhaps a Dogmatist more than anything else; Soranus was a Methodist; Aretaeus, a Pneumatist; Rufus and Galen were Eclectics. Some of their remedies are still in use, while many others have been superseded by more effective treatments; but some diseases and ailments with which they could not cope still baffle our medical men today.

We do not have to believe that the physicians of antiquity effected blood transfusions or employed electric shock treatments with the aid of the torpedo (electric eel).[8] Neither do we have to think that the best doctors used the remedies advocated by Pliny the Elder who would alleviate cancer with bear's grease, bull glue, and sow's brains or cure jaundice by a mixture of wine and the blood of an ass's foal. Bleeding, cupping, purging and vomiting, massaging, anointing and bathing, sweating and dieting, rocking with a cradle-like motion, and surgery were the most common treatments. Leeches were used; and, of course, there was an elaborate pharmacopeia.

Asclepiades said that it was the duty of the practitioner to treat the

patient safely, speedily, and pleasantly though Celsus warned that too
much haste and too much pleasure involved some danger. Celsus also
knew that anxiety and other things besides illness could excite the
pulse:[9]

> On this account a practitioner of experience does not seize a
> patient's forearm with his hand, as soon as he comes, but first
> sits down and with a cheerful countenance asks the patient how
> he finds himself; and if the patient has any fear, he calms him
> with entertaining talk, and only after that moves his hand to
> touch the patient.

Furthermore, "a practitioner should know above all which wounds
are incurable, which may be cured with difficulty, and which more
readily. For it is the part of a prudent man first not to touch a case he
cannot save, and not to risk the appearance of having killed one whose
lot is but to die." In addition, "a surgeon should be youthful or at any
rate nearer youth than age; with a strong and steady hand that never
trembles, and ready to use the left hand as well as the right; with vision
sharp and clear, and spirit undaunted; filled with pity so that he wishes
to cure his patient, yet not moved by his cries, to go too fast, or cut less
than is necessary; but he does everything just as if the cries of pain
cause him no emotion."

Galen pointed out that people may often pretend to be ill, and he
cited a number of instances from his own experience in which he was
able to see through deception. On one occasion[10] he had a case that
was a bit more complicated than the ordinary malingering. A woman
had insomnia. She had no fever and refused to answer any of his
questions about the symptoms accompanying her sleeplessness. Galen
concluded that she might have a "melancholy resulting from black
bile," or else she was troubled about some matter that she did not wish
to discuss. Following the sound procedure advocated by Rufus of
Ephesus, who said that not only the patient but also the other members
of the household should be questioned in order to build up a case
history, Galen interrogated the lady's maid and came to the conclusion
that melancholia must be ruled out. On a subsequent visit to the
patient, he noticed some agitation and an irregular pulse when someone
stopped by after the theatre to report that Pylades had danced that
day. The next day Galen arranged to have a visitor announce that
Morphus was dancing. This produced no reaction at all, but later, when
the name of Pylades was introduced, the patient once more showed
signs of excitement. Galen therefore diagnosed the lady's illness as a

pining for Pylades. He was able to verify his conclusion by discreet inquiries, but he does not tell us what he prescribed for the patient.

"The modes of mania are infinite in species," said Aretaeus,[11] "but one alone in genus. For it is altogether a chronic derangement of the mind, without fever." Both extrovert and introvert types seemed to be subject to the malady. Some appeared to be happy; others were dangerous; ingenious and docile persons produced "untaught astronomy, spontaneous philosophy, poetry truly from the muses." Uneducated persons might be good artificers or masons despite their mental derangement. Aretaeus knew a certain carpenter who was perfectly capable while at work, but mad as a hatter off the job. Some of the unfortunates had "extraordinary phantasies" — like the man who thought he was an adobe brick and refused to drink anything lest he dissolve.

The causes of mania, according to Soranus (Caelius Aurelianus),[12] were innumerable: severe hardship, injuries, the result of drinking love philtres, excesses, or overstudy. The philologist Artemidorus was startled by a crocodile; he subsequently believed that the reptile had chewed off his left leg and hand, and he lost his memory — "even of literature." Since Soranus was a Methodist, he diagnosed insanity as a form of stricture to be combatted by relaxation: light, warmth, quiet, massage, and warm water must be parts of the treatment. Visitors, especially strangers, were barred from the sickroom. In severe cases venesection, cupping of the head, and leeches should be used. During convalescence, the patient might be taken out in a sedan chair for "passive exercise." Subsequently, walking and vocal exercise might be prescribed, but the mind should be exercised, too. The patient should be made to answer questions and to proofread texts "marred by false statements"; later he should be encouraged to recite or deliver a discourse before an audience of friends. If the patient was unacquainted with literature, he might be given problems related to his occupation — on navigation, for example, if he was a pilot, and so on — or "let him play checkers." The other schools, of course, erred in their methods of treatment: by the use of cooling liquids or cold baths, sleep-producing drugs, or fasting, they simply increased the constriction. Unlike Aulus Gellius,[13] who thought that music could cure insanity as well as the gout and snake bite, the Methodists felt that the sound of music would congest the head.

The Dogmatists (no pun intended) had raised a question about the antiquity of hydrophobia. They said it was a new disease, but a careful search of the literature convinced the Methodists that Homer was acquainted with it.[14] Wherever there were dogs, there was bound to be hydrophobia. A Methodist or an Empiricist, sneered Rufus and Galen, could hardly treat anyone for hydrophobia since he would merely prescribe a remedy for dogbite without building up a case history. Celsus said that the poison must be drawn from the wound by cupping; this should be followed by cauterization, sweating, and the drinking of much wine. If this proved ineffectual after three days, and the patient showed a fear of water, there was just one thing to do: throw him into a tank until he had drunk his fill and lost his dread of the water. The Methodists prescribed relaxation by various means but doubted the efficacy of having the patient drink from a cup covered with the skin of a hyena. The best cure was that performed by the miracle-worker, Apollonius of Tyana,[15] who healed a lad of Tarsus who had suffered from hydrophobia for a whole month and was so far gone that he ran around on all fours barking like a dog. Apollonius located the mad canine who had bitten the youth and persuaded the animal to lick the boy's wound. The recovery was complete, and Apollonius graciously accorded an encore by curing the dog as well by forcing it to swim across a river. Apollonius explained his success in curing the boy by saying that, according to his diagnosis, the lad was possessed of the soul of Telephus, and thus he was induced to apply the principle of "the hair of the dog."

Pliny the Elder prescribed wine for cardiac ailments; the Methodists agreed but added rest and dieting. They regarded the disease as being one of looseness and relaxation. Pungent and astringent substances must therefore be used in large amounts. Ointments and plasters to reduce sweating were called for; a preparation made of Syrian sumach would restore strength to the esophagus.

"Refrigeration of the innate heat," said the Pneumatists, led to paralysis. This might come as the result of a wound, exposure to cold, indigestion, venery, or intoxication. For the Methodists, it was a case of constriction, of course. As recovery progressed, exercise of the paralyzed part was called for. In the case of the legs, a patient might begin exercises in a barber's chair which had supporting arms, or he might lean on a device of the kind "often built for babies learning to walk." Later, walking over hurdles and in and out of ditches might help; leaden weights could be added to the shoes to strengthen the muscles. Castor oil, swimming with an inflated bladder (not the patient's), and bathing at the spas of Padua, Vesuvius, Sena, and Caere was also beneficial. The waters of Avernus, near Naples, were also good for other kinds of constriction according to Martial,[16] for there was a lady named Laevina whose bathing there transformed her from a Penelope into a Helen, and she deserted her husband for a younger man.

Tetanus, said Aretaeus, might result from wounds or abortions. Women were more disposed toward tetanus than men because of their cold temperament, but they recovered more readily because the female is more humid than the male. In a bad case, the situation is hopeless: the doctor can only be sympathetic while people pray that the patient may soon be delivered by death.

Rufus of Ephesus knew that head injuries were serious and not immediately apparent. He cited the case of a Samian who had been hurt during a festival at which people chose up sides and threw stones at one another. This man was dazed after being struck on the head, but at first he seemed to recover. Twenty days later he had a relapse. Called in for consultation, Rufus got the case history and diagnosed the trouble as a skull fracture which he then remedied by an operation.

Colds and pulmonary diseases were common. Pliny the Elder would remedy catarrh by having the sufferer kiss a mule's nostrils; earthworms or boiled snails in raisin wine would do wonders for asthma. Said Aretaeus: [17]

> Animals live by two principal things, food and breath (pneuma); of these by far the most important is the respiration, for if it be stopped, the man will not endure long, but immediately dies.... The lungs contain the cause of attraction, for in the midst of them is situated a hot organ, the heart, which is the organ of life and respiration. It imparts to the lungs the desire of drawing in cold air, for it raises a heat in them.... If the lungs be affected, from a slight cause there is difficulty of breathing; the patient lives miserably, and death is the issue, unless someone effects a cure. But in a great affection, such as inflammation, there is a sense of suffocation, loss of speech and of breathing, and a speedy death. This is what we call Peripneumonia, being an inflammation of the lungs, with acute fever....

The remedy for "peripneumonia" was to open the veins at the elbow. This produced an evacuation of the veins which made more room in the lungs for the passage of the breath. The patient must also be purged with a mixture of natron, turpentine resin with honey, hyssop, and wild cucumber. Much the same concoction with the addition of mustard, iris root, and pepper was to be taken orally. Dry cupping could be applied to the back and shoulder, and beneficial foods were leeks, water cress, cabbage boiled in vinegar, and boiled spelt. The chest should be covered with wool soaked in oil and a mustard plaster. "When these things are done, if the disease do not yield, the patient is in a hopeless condition."

Diseased tonsils should be removed. They could be seized with a hook and excised with a scalpel; vinegar was recommended as an astringent for use after the operation. Hardened tonsils should be scratched round with the finger nail and drawn out.[18] Inflamed tonsils might lead to a form of synanche (choking). The essence of synanche was severe inflammation, "and this also serves to distinguish synanche from choking accomplished by a noose. For while this form of choking is also very swift and acute, it does not originate in an inflammation."[19]

Soranus and Celsus agreed that the extraction of a diseased tooth was a remedy of last resort. "Such removal is the loss of a part, not its cure." The infection should be first treated and cured, if possible, and then the tooth could be removed. Extraction was a risky business: the tooth might break off, the jaw might be dislocated, the eye damaged, or severe hemorrhage could follow the operation.

In the treatment of burns Celsus noted two stages: first, it was necessary to check the blisters and roughen the skin; second, healing was accomplished by soothing applications. In the beginning, lentil meal and honey, myrrh with wine, chalk and frankincense bark would work very well. This could be followed by flour mixed with rue, leek, or horehound. Healing might also be effected with lily, hound's tooth, or beet leaves boiled in wine and old oil.

It was customary to distinguish between acute and chronic diseases. In the former category were phrenitis, lethargy, apoplexy, epilepsy, tetanus, quinsey, pleurisy, hydrophobia, cholera, synanche, and satyriasis (a dreadful thing). Among the latter were dropsy, diabetes, dysentery, elephantiasis, and sciatica. Epilepsy was sometimes classified as a chronic disease rather than an acute one. Soranus also listed among the chronic diseases jaundice and incubus (nightmare). Phthisis, too, was naturally in the chronic category, and it is interesting to note in passing that Aretaeus prescribed rest and a milk diet as the best cure for this disease. Milk, agreed Plutarch[20] and Aretaeus, was a great food; nourishing, pleasant to take, sweet, mild, familiar from childhood, it was both a food and a medicine.

"Of chronic diseases," says Aretaeus, "the pain is great, the period of wasting long, and the recovery uncertain." The physician and patient must be courageous, and the former must persevere, find ways to vary the treatment, put on a show of optimism, and to indulge the patient in small, harmless things. In chronic diseases patients tended to avoid physicians; often they trusted more in amulets, incantations, or luck. This was most unfortunate: the worst thing that could be done was to postpone medical treatment, "for, by procrastination, they [the chronic diseases] pass into incurable affections, being of such a nature that they do not readily go off if they once attack; and if protracted by time, they will become strong, and end only in death." The patient should not be ashamed of his ailment nor shrink from fear of treatment. Some patients, ignorant of the final consequences, were content to live with the disease in its initial stages, "for since in most cases they do not die, so neither do they fear death, nor, for this reason, do they entrust themselves to the physician."[21]

In and out of the medical profession strange ideas were current regarding disease, the body, and bodily processes. Aulus Gellius noted the varying ideas of philosophers, physicians, and lawyers with regard to the period of gestation in human beings. The prevailing opinion in the second century, he said, was that a child was rarely born in the seventh month, never in the eighth, often in the ninth, and more often in the tenth. There was a case of an unfortunate woman who gave birth to a child in the eleventh month after her husband's death. According to the Twelve Tables, a child was supposed to be born in the tenth month; thus, not only was the child a doubtful heir, but there was also some doubt as to the propriety of its mother. The Emperor Hadrian however, after some research, decided that birth might actually and legitimately occur in the eleventh month. The authority of Homer was of some consequence since in *Od.* XI, 248-250 the god Poseidon predicted a twelve-month gestation period in the case of one of his own indiscretions. Moreover, Pliny the Elder cited an instance of a thirteen-month pregnancy.

There were also records of multiple births. Quintuplets were admitted to be rare although a case was known from the reign of Augustus in which, unfortunately, the five children and their mother all died. In the reign of Hadrian a woman was brought from Alexandria to Rome in order to display her quadruplets along with a fifth child born forty days after the original four. A Peloponnesian woman was said to have had quadruplets five times, while in Egypt it was reported that seven children in a single litter were not uncommon.

Laymen and even some doctors were often vague about anatomy no less an authority than the great Galen disappoints us in some aspect of his physiological knowledge.[22] Arteries which reach the skin, he says, draw in the outer air, while the interior arteries draw upon the heart. The veins take over something from the arteries and provide nutriment for the heart. Some parts of the body are properly nourished by thin, others by thick, blood.

Plague was a frightening thing. There seemed to be no way of dealing with it, and no one understood this better than the doctor who, like Galen, were very hard to find in plague times. Magic and faith alone could cope with these great disasters. Thus, Apollonius of Tyana[23] was worth any number of doctors when Ephesus was struck by plague. Encouraging the people, he led them to the theatre where he pointed out a beggar who was pretending to be blind. At the command of Apollonius the old fellow was surrounded by the Ephesians who showered him with stones. When the beggar showed some resentment, all were convinced that he was indeed the plague demon, and so many rocks were thrown that the victim was completely covered as by a cairn. When the stones were unpiled, the old man was gone; in his place was the wreck of a monstrous dog with foaming mouth now quite harmless since he had been beaten to a pulp.

The better doctors, of course, were violently opposed to magicians and magical cures. They especially resented the successful prognoses of Galen which savoured of the black art. How could anyone possibly predict to the moment the return of a fever or the turning point of an illness? After his spectacularly successful treatment of the philosopher Eudemus, Galen was warned that his competitors would defame him as a wizard and that his very life might be in danger; quite recently another promising young practitioner from the provinces had been found dead from poison.

A kind of apprentice system was basic to the medical education of the Pax Romana. Aspirants would attach themselves to some prominent doctor, attend his lectures, and follow him about town as he called on his patients. One of the best places for study was Alexandria where both Galen and Rufus of Ephesus profited from the rich Hellenistic medical tradition. Galen also confessed that he owed much to his father who saw to it that his son received a thorough grounding in literature, mathematics, and philosophy. The philosophical training Galen found valuable in several ways, one of them negative: he discovered the pitfalls of dialectic as far as proof was concerned and was henceforth careful to make use of demonstrations "of the geometrical character."[24] In addition to lecturing to their students, physicians also gave public lectures and demonstrations; these affairs could be pretty lively when hecklers and determined opponents challenged the speaker's views.

Oral instruction could be supplemented by information gleaned from a plethora of medical books on a variety of subjects. These books ranged all the way from a general handbook on medicine and surgery like that of Celsus to pamphlets on specific subjects. Soranus wrote a *Gynaecia* as well as long treatises on the acute and chronic diseases; the latter subjects were also treated by Aretaeus. Rufus of Ephesus wrote

"On the Interrogation of the Patient" and on the nomenclature of the parts of the body. Galen's works were numerous: he wrote on anatomy and physiology, dietetics and hygiene, pathology, diagnosis, therapeutics and surgery, and produced commentaries on Hippocrates and on the methods of the various "schools." Among the medical writers, paraphrasing, pirating, and plagiarism were common. Galen complained[25] that his works had been cannibalized by many writers and even taken over in their entirety by persons who claimed authorship for themselves. There exists some reason for doubt as to the originality of Celsus and Aretaeus; Galen himself did not always give credit where credit was due.

Galen felt that his book on anatomical procedure was better than most on this subject. In it he stressed the necessity of gaining anatomical knowledge from personal observation. At Alexandria where cadavers were still dissected by medical students, the opportunities for learning were best, but no one should neglect chance finds such as one might make in deserted graveyards or on the battlefield. If your luck was poor, you could always dissect an ape. "But even those apes most like human beings fall somewhat short of the absolutely erect posture. In them the head of the femur is adjusted somewhat obliquely to the hip-socket, and certain of the muscles which run down to the tibia come far forward; both of these factors impair or prevent assumption of the erect posture, as do also their feet, for in these the heels are somewhat narrow and the toes widely separated from each other."[26]

It is disappointing, but not surprising, to find that the medical writers of the Pax Romana had faults and characteristics common to other authors of the same period who dealt with rhetoric, oratory, grammar, law, and other subjects. A pervasive lack of originality, a predilection for disputation, a highly critical attitude where small details are concerned, and an increasing tendency to simplify and condense are frequently encountered; they are, in fact, the hallmarks of the age. Commentaries and commentaries upon commentaries seem to constitute the essence of scholarship. As in the earlier steps in education or in training for the law, the student wanted to progress rapidly and get it over with; thus, he was content with the barest minimum.

Galen and Plutarch were certainly justified in their feeling that an ounce of prevention was worth a pound of cure. A sound principle at any time, it was even more applicable in their age when the successful outcome of medical treatment was not to be taken for granted. If a man, said Plutarch, was moderate in all things, especially his diet and activities, he could hope to retain his health unimpaired. Galen was very proud of the fact that he had been free from illness for many years after his discovery of the "art of health." Individuals differed, however, and he would not venture to prescribe the same rules for everyone.

As ancient medicine approached its zenith in the second century A.D., as Dogmatist battered Empiricist, as Pneumatist scratched at Methodist, and as Galen berated them all, the muses steadfastly refused to desert the art which professed to have become a science. In the midst of all the turmoil, the public library in Rome received a precious gift, regrettably now lost, from Marcellus the Sidonian physician (otherwise unknown). This was the good doctor's own monograph on therapeutics. Entitled the *Chrinodes,* it covered the subject in forty books of heroic verse![27]

FOOTNOTES

1. *Correspondence of Marcus Aurelius Fronto,* ed. and trans. by C. R. Haines, Loeb Classical Texts, 2 vols., London and New York 1919.

2. Marcus Aurelius, *Meditations,* I, 16.

3. Reprinted by permission of the publishers from C. R. Haines, *Marcus Cornelius Fronto,* Cambridge, Mass.: Harvard University Press, 1919. The passage is from Vol. I, p. 197.

4. E. Dupouy, *Médicine et moeurs de l'ancienne Rome d'après les poètes latins,* Paris 1892, p. 292.

5. Athenaeus, *Deipnosophistae,* XV, 666.

6. For a good account, see T. C. Allbutt, *Greek Medicine in Rome,* London 1921.

7. Galen, *Order of his own Books,* XIX. Translated by A. J. Brock, *Greek Medicine,* London 1929, p. 180. Reprinted by permission of E. P. Dutton & Co., Inc., New York.

8. Dupuoy, *op. cit.,* p. 152 and 163; Lucan, *Pharsalia,* VI, 630; Pliny, *Natural History,* XXXVIII, 50.

9. Celsus, *De Medicina,* III, 6, 6. Reprinted by permission of the publishers from W. G. Spencer, *Celsus,* Cambridge, Mass.: Harvard University Press, 1948. The passage will be found in Vol. I, p. 255.

10. Galen, *Prognosis,* VI.

11. *Extant Works of Aretaeus the Cappadocian,* ed. and trans. by F. Adams, London 1856 (Sydenham Society Publication, no. 28), pp. 103-104.

12. *Caelius Aurelianus,* ed. and trans. by I. E. Drabkin, Chicago 1950, p. 537 and 559. This fifth century translation by Aurelianus is our principal source for Soranus.

13. Aulus Gellius, *Attic Nights,* IV, 13.

14. Aurelianus, *op. cit.*, p. 387.
15. Philostratus, *Life of Apollonius*, VI, 43.
16. Martial, *Epigrams*, I, 62.
17. Aretaeus, *op. cit.*, pp. 261-262; see also p. 419.
18. Celsus, *De Medicina*, VII, 12.
19. Aurelianus, *op. cit.*, p. 303.
20. Plutarch, *Rules for the Preservation of Health.*
21. Aretaeus, *op. cit.*, p. 294 and 457.
22. Galen, *Natural Faculties,* III, 15.
23. Philostratus, *Life of Apollonius,* IV, 10.
24. Brock, *Greek Medicine,* p. 179.
25. Galen, *On his own Books,* Kühn XIX, p. 8 ff.
26. Brock, *op. cit.*, p. 162.
27. *Greek Anthology, Sepulchral Epigrams,* no. 158.

A Polite Occupation

Historians are a lazy crew.

Juvenal

MARTIAL KNEW A DABBLER who did many things prettily, but nothing well.[1] This versatile dilettante of Martial's declaimed, appeared as an advocate in the courts, wrote poetry, produced mimes, penned epigrams, strummed on the lyre, played ball, and studied the heavens. He also wrote history.

Other Romans of this age "also wrote history." That was the trouble: physicians, lawyers, and teachers were professional men, but the historians were amateurs. Unlike rhetoric, philosophy, law, or medicine, history was not a subject for which formal training was available. There was no money in historical writing, either. *"Quis dabit historico quantum daret acta legenti?"* queried Juvenal.[2] Who indeed will give to the historian as much as he gives to the man "who reads out the news?" Reflecting upon the salaries of some telecasters of today's events, the modern historian may feel that he has discovered a new constant among the variables of his science.

However peaceful the Pax Romana may have been in its military aspects, there was a spate of activity on its intellectual battlefields. No Peace of God, no truce of an Olympic year, interrupted the hostilities of scholarship. In this quarrelsome age, therefore, it is remarkable to discover that people almost universally agreed on two points: that the study of history was useful, and that practically anyone could write history if he could find the time for it. And they proved themselves dead wrong on both counts.

A work of history may be directly the product of its age, or it may be the product of a cultural accumulation. In the time of Herodotus, for example, precedents for historical writing were anything but well established. When Herodotus began to write, the two major developments in the fifth century had been the victory over the Persians and the rise of the Athenian Empire. For his subject Herodotus chose the former, possibly because he was not an Athenian, but probably because of the popularity of the Homeric tradition that emphasized the hostility of Greek and barbarian. With regard to form and concept, Herodotus certainly followed Homer.[3] He produced an heroic epic in prose which was Homeric even in its frequency of digression; actually, the digressions were a matter more of convenience or necessity rather than of imitation since the history, like the *Iliad* or the *Odyssey,* was intended to be recited rather than read. Just as Herodotus took Homer as his model because of the literary preëminence of Homer in that age, so also the current Greek interest in geography and ethnology led Herodotus to preface his history with a lengthy introduction which surveyed the peoples and countries of the known world. Moreover, the moralizing of Herodotus was quite in keeping with the tastes and preferences of his contemporaries.

The rationalist Athenian Thucydides was determined to avoid what he conceived to be the mistakes of Herodotus. The Father of History had demonstrated to everyone the difficulty of getting at the past. In an age devoid of libraries, in a period of scattered records, it would have been virtually impossible to deal with the remote past in the kind of history that Thucydides proposed to write. He had been exposed to the full tide of the new learning which stressed methodology, observation, and scientific accuracy. Therefore Thucydides chose to write current history, and this meant that he would take as his subject the Peloponnesian War in which he had been a participant. The influence of the drama upon the form of Thucydides' history is obvious; we can also see mirrored in his work the rising popularity of oratory, while the inclusion of two dialogues also reflects contemporary literary developments.

Throughout the rest of antiquity, mere chroniclers excepted, the writers of history tended to use either Herodotus or Thucydides as their models. The two founders of history were alike in their belief that history should be didactic, that it was therefore useful, and that men could profit from the lessons of the past. They also agreed that history was a form of literature; therefore, the writing of history was an art: the finished product should be literary in concept, form, and style.

On the other hand, Thucydides introduced "science" into historical research. The historian should search out and seek to establish the truth; he should not be like Herodotus who was content merely to report varying accounts or "accept the first opinion that came to hand." In addition, the approach of Thucydides was essentially impersonal; he dealt with nations or states and trends and seldom with individuals and their personalities.

Thucydides brought the writing of history to its highest point of perfection in antiquity. None of his successors was fortunate enough to possess the same rare combination of abilities that had produced simultaneously an artist and a scientist. Lesser mortals must be content to write either scientific or literary history. In a way, it might be said that Thucydides ruined history by setting up a conflict between science and art. His impersonality repelled the many and attracted only the few; it encouraged almost immediately the rise of biography which did, of course, concern itself with individuals. Subsequent historians were forced to choose whether they would cater to the serious or the popular interest, and the writing of history degenerated into two forms: scientific history which, with the increase and preservation of records, the development of libraries, and the spread of book-learning or scholarship, tended to be dry, dessicated, and impotent; and literary history which, written to be read rather than studied, was more often than not "attractive at truth's expense."

By the Hellenistic Age the expansion of literacy, the growth of geographical knowledge, the profound political changes that exalted the empire over the city state, a multiplication of records and documents, and an immense complexity of culture and interests all had their effects upon the writing of history. People produced universal, national, and local histories; some wrote the history of military affairs, strategy, art, oratory, or literature; there were annalists, there were biographers, and here were geographers who described countries and peoples. The size of the historian's audience had increased, and thus there was a greater demand for both popular and scholarly works.

Polybius, the best of the Hellenistic historians, was an intellectual whose experience in public affairs averted from him the curse of scholarship. He could be a scientific historian in the best sense at a time when for others the "science" of history had become mere methodology. Polybius was convinced of the didactic value of history, and he also chose a great topic of current interest, the rise of Rome, for his theme; it was only a deficiency on the literary side that prevented him from attaining the stature of a Thucydides. Critical of other historians, pamphleteer at heart, and with an Aristotelian interest in describing and categorizing political institutions, Polybius was clearly a product of his age. One of the principles which he stressed again and again, however, was not typical of the Hellenistic period, for Polybius insisted that book-learning must be supplemented by practical experience and real knowledge of the world: research could not be confined to books.

So far, then, had the discipline of history evolved when the Romans came into contact with the Greeks. The Romans had before them the models constructed by Herodotus and Thucydides and the examples and the varieties of history produced in the fourth century and the

Hellenistic Age. Yet the fine points always eluded the Romans: they paid lip service to the idea that the historian must be truthful, they understood that history might be scientific or literary, they recognized the different categories of historical periods and subjects, and they were convinced of the didactic value of history, but there never was a Roman Thucydides. Furthermore, by the time the Romans were exposed to the full influence of Greek culture, they had developed a tradition of historical writing of their own which was to be very influential and persistent.

At the end of the third century B.C., when the Romans began to write about their past, their first efforts were couched in the form of heroic epics or the barest of annals. The epics were composed under the spell of Homer and the influence of the Greek historical epics, while the prose annals were brief and topical because of the form of the public and private records which were used as sources. The epic treatment was long-lived; it survived in works like Lucan's *Pharsalia* or was sublimated as in Virgil's *Aeneid,* but it also influenced the prose writers. Another influence on historical prose derived from oratory, a form of great importance to the Romans and very highly regarded by them from early times. Thus, as the annalistic tradition developed, it tended to borrow from the epic and to make great use of speeches in lieu of exposition. When the so-called younger annalists succeeded the older annalists about 120 B.C., historical works became longer and fuller mainly because the bare skeleton of the annals was now padded with speeches. Livy, the youngest annalist, represents the culmination and consolidation of the annalistic, epic, and oratorical traditions.

Other features which became characteristic of Roman historical writing may be found in the works of Sallust. A Caesarian in his politics, Sallust had had a career of sorts in public life before he was forced to retire and occupy his leisure with historical composition. The subjects which he chose to treat were certainly worthy of attention – the Jugurthine War, the history of the period 78-67 B.C., and the conspiracy of Catiline – but they appealed especially to Sallust because these were periods in which for the most part the popular party shone to advantage while the conservatives were in disgrace or eclipse. In short, Sallust had an axe to grind: he was a political pamphleteer. Concerned with political and military events and personalities, Sallust included many vivid pen portraits of the actors in his history, and he used many speeches. He makes good reading, but his carelessness about chronology and his lack of impartiality show that he was not a scientific, nor even a professional, historian. His was primarily literary history as was also the work of Livy.

If we set Sallust and Livy side by side we soon discover that they have more in common than their concept of history as a literary genre and their unprofessional disregard of accuracy and detail. Both emphasize personalities; both are concerned with military and political affairs; both write with a particular audience in mind. Sallust is obviously tendentious, but it has also been suspected that Livy's treatment of the first century B.C. was mildly partisan.[4] Both writers, perhaps under the influence of oratory, often employ an epigrammatic or sententious style which is memorable and effective.[5] Who can forget Livy's characterization of Cicero which ends with the judgement that Cicero was, after all, a great man "whose praise it would need a Cicero to extoll?" Or Sallust's portrait of Sempronia who could do many things better than a lady should? Finally, both writers believed that history taught by example, and both stressed the theme of national degeneration.

Cultural accumulation can go far in explaining the kind of historical writing that was done under the principate. The historians of this era were heirs to the Greek past: they read Herodotus and Thucydides, they were willing to concede the virtues of the scientific method even though they might be too lazy to use it, and they were familiar with the various approaches or divisions of history which had developed after Thucydides. In addition to the Greek past, however, there was now the Roman past which exerted a considerable influence upon those who wrote in Latin; Tacitus, as will appear, was heir to both the Greek and Roman traditions. Moreover, by the Age of Cicero, and certainly under the principate, historical literature was bi-lingual, and it is neither practical nor always possible to separate the Greeks from the Romans.

Many kinds and varieties of history were being written from the Ciceronian Age onward through the principate. Quintus Curtius Rufus and Arrian, for example, wrote about Philip and Alexander; Pliny the Elder and Tacitus chose to deal with the area of Germany, while the Sicilian Diodorus composed a universal history. There were continuators of Livy, and there were people who wrote histories of strategy, architecture, art, philosophy, and the like. There were historians, antiquarians, and biographers; people also wrote memoirs and auto-biographies. It was inevitable, too, that history should be affected by the prevailing trend toward compilation and condensation. Livy's work, excellent though it might be, was too long for busy people to read and too bulky to be accommodated in most libraries,[6] so it was condensed into an epitome. Diodorus had already seen the advantage of an encyclopedic history, a synthesis of knowledge, a package deal, a multivitamin capsule which the reader might swallow without pain or effort. The successors of Diodorus refined his idea; by the fourth century the whole of Roman history could be compressed into a few pages by epitomizing epitomes, and the reader could read in a few minutes what the writer had been able to copy out in a few hours.

The value of a knowledge of history or of the study of the discipline was rarely questioned. Most agreed with Diodorus that history could give the young the wisdom of the aged, that one could profit from the mistakes of others without having to suffer the pain of learning the hard way by personal experience. History inspired the emulation of great men and deterred its readers from evil doing; it fostered patriotism and morality. History preserved the memory of individuals: it gave a kind of immortality to great men of the past and also to the historians who wrote about them. History, said Diodorus, is the mistress of eloquence. Cicero and Quintilian agreed that it could be helpful both to the orator and the lawyer. Certain historians — Herodotus, Thucydides, Sallust, and Livy — could be studied for their literary style as well as for content.[7]

The craft of the historian came in for somewhat less discussion in these later times than it had in the Hellenistic Age. The day of the professional historian was pretty well past. While most writers did not omit the customary platitudes about the necessity and difficulty of getting at the truth, Josephus[8] was one of the few who had much to say about methods and standards. Plutarch's essay on the malignity of Herodotus scarcely comes under the heading of historical criticism, nor are the comments of Dionysius of Halicarnassus on the merits of Herodotus, Thucydides, Xenophon, Philistus, and Theopompus much more mature. Dionysius preferred Herodotus to Thucydides not only because the former chose the more suitable and glorious subject for his history but also because he handled it more adeptly by emphasizing the good and criticizing or omitting the bad, by employing digression instead of wearying the reader by plowing through from beginning to end, and, moreover, by choosing a suitable point both to begin and to end his work. The prevailing taste of the age may also be indicated by the fact that Dionysius expressed a preference for Timaeus over Polybius. This suggests a possible reaction against the "scientific" variety of history.

Many famous historians and biographers flourished in the age of the Pax Romana. Among them were Arrian, Appian, Florus, Plutarch, and Suetonius, but Cornelius Tacitus is conceded to outrank all the rest. There is no doubt of it, the *Annals* and *Histories* of Tacitus make fascinating reading. He possessed marvelous powers of description and great narrative skill, but as a historian Tacitus seems to have had his faults. Rated as careful but not methodical, Tacitus did not make the fullest use of public documents nor was he always precise about details of geography and military affairs. He was not completely consistent in the portrayal of character, and he was anything but detached and impartial in the Thucydidean manner.[9] Nothing so obvious as the greatness of Tacitus can be denied, however; it may be much more profitable to speculate as to why he wrote as he did. Was the work of Tacitus the product of his age, or was it the product of cultural accumulation?

When Tacitus began to write history in the days of the first Good Emperors, it was fashionable to say that the Romans had just escaped from tyranny into the happy realm of liberty. The senatorial aristocracy, the class which had suffered most from the Julio-Claudians and the Flavians, took a special delight in castigating the early emperors. Suetonius in his biographies of the twelve Caesars exploited this sentiment to the full, and it was perfectly natural for Tacitus, as a senator and as an author, to do the same thing. Moreover, the popularity of satire was at its height; to assure ourselves of this we have only to recall the names of Petronius, Persius, Juvenal, Martial, and Lucian or to remember the *Apocolocyntosis* of Seneca. Satire, then, was a weapon which Tacitus could use in attacking the memory of the bad, but now harmless, emperors. In his pages the satirist more than once runs away with the historian.[10]

On the other hand, it is not hard to show that Tacitus was a historian very much in the Roman tradition. Tendentious and sententious, emphasizing personalities, politics, and military events, trained as an orator and therefore under the influence of oratory, playing on the theme of national degeneration and definitely a literary historian, Tacitus displayed many of the traits equally characteristic of Sallust or Livy. Like Sallust, he had been active in public affairs, and, like Sallust, he certainly had an axe to grind.

Nevertheless, Tacitus was not completely divorced from the older Greek tradition. His first work, the *Histories,* dealt with the story of his own age; thus, like Thucydides, his first concern was with current history. Thucydides and Polybius would have approved of the practical experience and knowledge of affairs that Tacitus brought to his task. He was orthodox in his belief in the didactic value of history. Furthermore, the work of Tacitus, like that of Herodotus, was designed to be publicly declaimed or recited.[11]

All this is pretty much on the surface. It does not explain how Tacitus, the public official, the distinguished orator, the famous advocate, came to be a historian. Neither does it explain fully why

Tacitus wrote as he did at this particular time. For the answers to sucl
questions as these we shall have to dig much deeper.

It seems fairly safe to assume that Tacitus did not begin his career a
a writer until he reached middle age. In order to date the *Dialogus,* hi
first work, as late as the middle nineties, we do not need to concur witl
the opinion of Syme that this dialogue on oratory shows a writer whe
has turned his back on eloquence and begun to think like a historian. I
may well have been the success of this admirable work, however, tha
persuaded Tacitus to produce the semi-biographical *Agricola* and th
semi-historical *Germania* about A.D. 98. Like Cassius Dio, who wa
encouraged by the warm reception accorded his first tentative efforts to
try something much more ambitious, Tacitus had now found the rang
and was able to score a direct hit with his *Histories* which covered th
period 69-96 A.D. By 105 the early books of this work were well unde
way, and the whole was completed by 109. The *Annals,* dealing wit
events from the death of Augustus to the Year of the Four Emperors
was a natural extension backward from the *Histories* to include thos
other tyrants, the Julio-Claudians, with the Flavians. The first books c
the *Annals* were written by 117 A.D.; the work was finished by 123. *
After this Tacitus began to write, but never finished, a history of th
reigns of Nerva and Trajan.

When Tacitus was writing the *Histories,* his friend Pliny the Younge
supplied him with two "first hand" accounts of the eruption c
Vesuvius which had occurred in 79 A.D. When we reflect that Pliny
who had literary aspirations of his own, was writing *for publication* th
story of something that had taken place at least twenty years earlier, w
cannot feel that we possess in these letters a primary source in the idea
sense. We should certainly, at any rate, know much more about Tacitu
as a historian if we possessed the part of the *Histories* in which h
treated the catastrophe at Pompeii. How did Tacitus make use of th
information provided by Pliny? Did he consult other accounts or othe
eye witnesses?

Even so, Pliny's remarks are revealing, to say the least. Tacitus, h
says, will immortalize the name of the elder Pliny by including it in hi
history. Tacitus will select what is most suitable from the younge
Pliny's account because there is *certainly* a big difference between
letter and a history, or between writing to a friend and writing for a
audience! Tacitus, of course, will also read the second letter, "so fa
beneath the dignity of a history," without any notion of using it as :
stands! Somewhat later, convinced that the works of Tacitus will b
immortal, Pliny pleads for a footnote that will insure his own fame. H
wishes Tacitus to take special notice of certain proceedings of th

Senate which displayed Pliny in no unfavorable light. Tacitus can
hardly have overlooked this episode, but Pliny wants to be sure that his
friend misses none of its implications. Naturally, Pliny will not
encourage Tacitus to go beyond the bounds of reality because history
should never desert the truth. Pliny shows in another letter that the
historian who dealt with the contemporary was under considerable
pressure to make additions or deletions. Tacitus must have had his
problems!

Even Pliny himself toyed momentarily with the idea of writing
history. Many people had urged him to try it. His own personal
modesty forbade him to think that he would be successful, but he
confessed that his desire for this kind of immortal fame was almost
irresistible. And history, after all, was much easier to write than poetry;
people had high standards for orators and poets, but they were more
lenient with historians. Pliny was too busy to start on the history right
away or even to make a decision about such a project, but he would be
happy to have suggestions about possible historical topics. Should he
deal with the present or the past? It really did not matter. Either choice
would involve more inconvenience than difficulty. If he chose to write
about the past, he would have merely to collate the works of his
predecessors; this would be a nuisance and a bore, but the spade work
would have been done for him. If he chose the present for his subject,
he would run the risk of offending many people and pleasing only a
few. We are left with the impression, however, that Pliny was willing to
take that chance. In his letters to Tacitus he had already shown that he
was no grubbing antiquarian: Pliny's interests were in his own times —
and in himself.

One cannot read this letter of Pliny's to Capito without being
reminded of what Cicero says in the *Laws*. [13] Cicero had been urged to
write history "in order that Rome might rival Greece" in this
department. It was the duty of Cicero to glorify Rome — the greatness
of Rome was a theme attractive to Livy, Dionysius, Florus, and Appian,
too. Should Cicero begin with the earliest times? Certainly not! The
most important events had occurred in his own generation. The career
of Pompey must be suitably treated, and Cicero would not be averse to
writing about his own consulship (again). The writing of history
required a long period of leisure; it was something that could not be
interrupted and then picked up again. The project would have to wait
for Cicero's retirement.

Cicero would probably have agreed with Aulus Gellius [14] that
ἱστορία meant a knowledge of current events. Also history, according to
Cicero, [15] was a narrative written in an ornate style "with here and

there a description of a country or a battle" and studded with "occasional harangues and exhortations." A knowledge of history was handy thing for an orator;[16] while Cicero implies that current history should omit no detail, historical works dealing with past ages were mos admirable when brief and to the point — like the *Liber Annalis* o Atticus which must have been a real potboiler.[17]

Potboiler, pamphlet, propaganda, and (personal) panegyric were to certain extent synonymous in Roman historiography as far as mos people were concerned. Josephus was not far wrong when h complained of the tendentiousness of his day. It was also no wonde that he felt compelled to remind his readers that historical research di not consist of the mere rearrangement of older materials but rather i the discovery of new evidence which in itself would justify a new treatment of the chosen subject.[18]

The naive theory that just anybody could write history should have been, but was not, exploded by the full but unmistakable thud of major historical flop —Fronto's account of the Parthian war conducted by Lucius Verus. The gay and irresponsible colleague of Marcu Aurelius had arranged to provide Fronto, his old teacher, with all th despatches, letters, and documents relating to the campaign. Th important generals serving under Verus were also instructed to draw u memoranda as grist for Fronto's mill. With Thucydides as one of hi models, Fronto was supposed to dwell upon the early failures of th Romans before the hero's arrival at the front.

Fronto did his best, but he admitted that this was the tale of a Achilles in need of a Homer. The army was in a sad state, yet Verus, b his energy and example, restored discipline and morale. It was later sai that Verus expended most of his energies and set most of his example in skirmishes with dancing girls at Antioch, but there is no suggestion c this in Fronto. Warlike in contrast to the peace-loving Hadrian, clemen in contrast to the harsh Trajan, Verus was a great leader who overcam the Parthians completely and utterly, a feat that no other Roman ha ever been able to accomplish. It was a new Jugurthine War. Fronto wa a great admirer of Sallust, and it is perfectly clear that he borrowe from his model both in style and presentation; it would be kinder no to mention the phrases and sentences borrowed in their entirety.

About this time, Lucian, who had previously withered philosopher sophists, rhetoricians, and other poseurs with his satire, now turned hi belated attention to the historians with a helpful little treatise entitle *How to Write History*. The current rash of historical composition, h said, reminded him of something that had happened long ago at Abder when a strange epidemic had affected the whole population of th town. People had wandered about reciting lines from Greek tragedy, particularly the *Andromeda* of Euripides, until the fever was broken by a sharp frost. The apparent cause of the malady was that, during the hot weather, the people had attended a memorable performance of the *Andromeda* in the local theatre and contracted the fever there with the result that the play and the heat had been too much for them. Now, said Lucian, the fever had struck again, but this time the war with Parthia was the agent of the disease and had set everyone to writing history. Lucian himself was unaffected, but he felt out of place. Like the philosopher Diogenes at the time when everyone at Corinth was bustling around preparing for the defense of the town against Philip, Lucian would simulate activity by rolling his tub: he would give advice on how history ought to be written.

Lucian was disappointed to find that no one seemed to think instruction was necessary. The ability to write history was a natural gift, people said; it was just like talking, seeing, or eating. Lucian felt that history should not be confused with panegyric, poetry, or eulogy. He then went on to make criticisms of what he claimed were some of the current productions: one writer "compared our ruler to Achilles," another author emulated Thucydides, others wrote brilliant prefaces and followed with the history itself as a kind of appendix, and still others seemed to know very little about geography or military affairs; the almost inevitable funeral oration frequently turned up, and many of the titles of these masterpieces of history were longer than the histories themselves.

After discoursing on these defects and giving other examples of things which the historian ought to avoid, Lucian then outlines the ideal qualifications and methods appropriate for a writer of history. The historian should possess political insight and facility of expression; the former a man had to have from birth, but the latter might be acquired. The historian should be honest and experienced in political and military affairs; he should have some of the poetic spirit; and he should gather his facts carefully, organize them, and make an outline of what he wished to say. Much more is said about the actual process of composition; most of it is extremely sensible, for Lucian seems in dead earnest here. He makes no secret of his admiration for Thucydides, and he ends by exhorting the historian to write, not for the moment, but for posterity.

This was a far cry from the sentiments of Fronto who thought that history should be written in the grand style, or Quintilian who regarded history as a poem unfettered by metre.[19] Too many people were of the opinion that history could or should be written in the same way that

Pliny advised Caninius[20] to write his poem on the Dacian War of Trajan. Too many writers of history, as Herodian said, were content to seek renown as literary stylists or to arouse interest through scandal-mongering or iconoclasm. Too often the rhetor got the best of the historian and distorted history in order to give more point to his narrative.[21]

The failure of the Pax Romana to produce a truly great historian may in itself have a historical explanation. The Roman tradition of historical writing with its emphasis on the literary side and its bent for pamphleteering and partisanship did not encourage the best in historiography, but there is discernible the shadow of another tradition which might be even more baneful in its effect. This is the tradition of the "polite occupation."

In the days of the Scipionic Circle many prominent Romans had taken an interest in Greek culture. The introduction of this culture into Rome and its elucidation was something in which a gentleman might engage himself as a kind of avocation or hobby without compromising his social status. In the first century B.C. philosophy, but more particularly the study of oratory, became a polite occupation. Oratory was vital and essential in the days of the dying republic, but not everyone agreed with Cicero and Caesar that it was necessary to go abroad to study oratory. Some very successful orators did not feel impelled to write treatises on oratory or to pass around their speeches for criticism among their friends as Cicero and others did. The notorious excursions of Cicero and Caesar in pursuit of the muse as well as the complaints of Horace in the *Ars Poetica* show that writing poetry was also a hobby. And historical composition was clearly in the same category.

Under the principate the Romans continued to indulge in these polite occupations, but there were some shifts in the relative popularity of the various activities. As the emphasis in philosophy became more and more concentrated on ethics and philosophy assumed the character of a religion or a substitute for religion, the study of philosophy became a serious matter and less of a hobby. Oratory, on the other hand, lost its vitality; it was not taken as seriously under the principate as under the republic, and a certain cynicism developed which further lowered its prestige even among the polite occupations. Amateurs continued to compose poetry and to criticize the poetry written by others, but sensible people were now ready to admit the superiority of the professionals.

This left history. Lucian's satire by itself would not be convincing evidence, but, combined with the testimony of Pliny and Fronto, it suggests that history was the most popular of the polite occupations of the Pax Romana. It may also have enjoyed the greatest prestige. It can hardly be a matter of coincidence that so many historical or biographical works have survived from this age. No other period in Roman history can match its roster in numbers: Arrian, Appian, Fronto, Florus, Plutarch, Suetonius, Tacitus, and — by stretching the chronology a bit — Cassius Dio and Herodian. Our list includes senators, consulars, civil servants, orators, rhetors, and philosophers, but there is not a professional historian in the lot.

It is not hard to see how Tacitus got into history; in another age he might have remained an orator. We need not regret that his lost or unfinished history of Nerva and Trajan is unavailable: without his usual satire and invective, which he would scarcely have dared to employ in his case, Tacitus would make poor reading.

FOOTNOTES

1. Martial, *Epigrams,* II, 7.
2. Juvenal, *Satires,* VII, 104.
3. Dionysius of Halicarnassus, *Letter to Pompeius,* III.
4. M. L. W. Laistner, *Greater Roman Historians,* Berkeley 1947, pp. 1-82.
5. On the pointed style, see M. Hadas, *Stoic Philosophy of Seneca,* New York 1958, p. 17.
6. Martial, *Epigrams,* XIV, 190.
7. Dionysius, *op. cit.,* III and Quintilian, *Institutes,* X, 1.
8. Josephus, *Jewish War,* I, 1.
9. On Tacitus, see R. Syme, *Tacitus,* 2 vols., Oxford 1958 and Laistner, *op. cit.*
10. Laistner, *op. cit.,* p. 139.
11. *Ibid.,* p. 137.
12. Syme, *op. cit.,* Vol. II, pp. 768-82.
13. Pliny, *Letters,* II, 62.
14. Aulus Gellius, *Attic Nights,* V, 18.
15. Cicero, *Orator,* 66.
16. Cicero, *De Oratore,* I, 18, 201.
17. Cicero, *Brutus,* III, 13-14.
18. Josephus, *Jewish War,* I, 1 ff.
19. Quintilian, *Institutes,* X, 1, 31.
20. Pliny, *Letters,* VIII, 4.
21. Cicero, *Brutus,* X, 42.

9

Schizophrenic Science

It seems fitting that an educated man should be acquainted with these facts as well.

Aelian

FROM A VERY EARLY PERIOD the folk literature of the Near East included a story about a huge fish that swallowed a man. The tale was so popular that it got into the Old Testament, and Lucian, who was steeped in Oriental lore, used the theme in his *True History* where he turned it into the biggest fish story of all time. Lucian and his imitators, including a fellow named Rudyard Kipling, do not seem to have been in earnest about the piscatorial marvels which they described, but there were people living under the Pax Romana who were quite serious when they themselves discussed the wonders of the finny deep. The Isaac Waltons of antiquity knew that the best way to catch a sargue was to disguise oneself as a goat; male mullets or parrot wrasses could be caught by using the female of the species as bait — these varieties were shamefully wanton; flute playing would lure crabs onto the land where they could be taken with facility; certain crabs which flew like grasshoppers were fairly easy to snare, and their meat was extremely good for sciatica. Whales were amphibious; they often came ashore to warm themselves in the sun. Seneca had heard of a great encounter between dolphins and crocodiles at one of the mouths of the Nile; the gentleness and amiability of the dolphin was almost proverbial, but in his ancient Battle of the Nile the crocodiles got the worst of it. Aelian and Pliny failed to agree about oysters: Aelian said that pearls were generated when lightning flashed upon the oyster shell, but Pliny maintained that lightning inhibited the growth of pearls and that thunder would produce a miscarriage. Apuleius' interest in ichthyology got him into trouble in North Africa when he dissected a sea hare.[1] People accused him of being a magician, but Apuleius claimed he was only trying to investigate this curious fish. It was well known that sea hares were dangerously inedible, but one wonders whether Apuleius was suspected of being a Christian.

The reptilian world was no less fascinating. Lucian, as usual, was hard to beat because he knew of some reversible snakes in Africa which had a head at each end and could proceed in either direction.[2] Lizards were just about indestructible: the severed parts of a lizard would reunite, and, if blinded, the creature would regain its sight. Aelian and Pliny concurred about the viper's mating habits; they agreed that the male inserted his head in the mouth of the female and that she was accustomed to decapitate her lover in an excess of rapture. The farther one proceeded from the civilized world, the larger and more venomous the serpents became. Aulus Gellius[3] had heard of a snake in Africa that was one hundred and twenty feet in length; out in India, of course, snakes were nothing less than horrendous: some were so big that they just reached up and caught high flying birds. It was bad enough close to home since the basilisk was indigenous to Cyrene, and Egypt was simply crawling with poisonous reptiles. The land of the pharaohs was spared one plague, however, because its frontiers were policed by the black ibis which averted sneak attacks by winged serpents.

Speaking of birds, a real marvel was the phoenix which visited Egypt every five hundred years and spent the rest of its time in India except when it was roosting on its nest of spices at the source of the Nile.[4] The phoenix was certainly not a figment of the imagination because Pliny knew of one that had been displayed in Rome as part of the celebration attending the eight hundredth birthday of the city. The bird had a built-in chronometer and knew how to calculate five hundred years without the aid of an abacus.

Somewhat more common than the phoenix, but no less remarkable was the bee-eater, the antique variety of the whiffenpoof, which always flew backwards. There were no male vultures in the second century; all vultures were female and were impregnated by the south wind for which purpose they had sense enough to turn around and open their beaks when the wind blew from that quarter. Vulture's eggs, moreover, always came in bakers' dozens. When Menippus made his famous excursion into outer space,[5] he employed the right wing of an eagle and the left wing of a vulture because of the well-known flying power of these birds. Cranes were good fliers, too, but they always proceeded in formation and rested their beaks on one another's tail feathers. Cranes and bees were accustomed to carry stones as ballast in flight. Parenthetically, things were generally better managed in ancient times than now, because the hives were all ruled by *king* bees.

Modern zoology seems not to have learned many facts about the animal kingdom that were almost in the category of the commonplace in the second century. Goats breathe through their ears; hyaenas alternate their sex year by year; elephants climb trees; locusts in India are so large that their legs, when dried, can be used as saws; no donkey will bray if you tie a stone to his tail. Nereids and Tritons used to haunt the coasts of Iberia where they terrorized sailors and landlubbers, too. Pausanias saw a pickled Triton in Greece.[6]

Monkeys, apes, dogs, horses, and elephants were believed to be particularly intelligent. Plutarch,[7] Pliny, and Aelian had much to say about this. The elephant was regarded as sensible, clever, and affectionate. One of the beasts, when scolded by its trainer for its slowness in learning a trick, was found in the dead of night diligently practising. Pliny knew of an elephant that learned to write Greek, while Aelian recorded the case of an elephant that could write Latin. The devoutness of elephants was beyond question: they worshipped both the sun and the moon. The longevity of pachyderms was known to everyone, but few people were aware of the existence of an old elephants' home at the foot of the Atlas Mountains. This bit of information was not lost with the passing centuries, for it did not escape the attention of Edgar Rice Burroughs or H. Rider Haggard. Various stories about particular animals were told over and over. The tale of the amorous dolphin was a great favorite: it was used by the two Plinys, Plutarch, Aulus Gellius, and, of course, Aelian.[8] Bucephalus got quite a work-out,[9] and Androcles and the lion, or a reasonable facsimile, was still another repeater.[10]

There were certain people in the second century A.D. — or the first, too, for that matter — who found it hard to believe some of the nature lore uncovered by earnest researchers. Even Aulus Gellius had his moments of skepticism. Fed up with tales of the marvelous, he turned to Pliny's *Natural History* where, to his dismay, he found more of the same.[11] The work of Pliny was so well documented that poor Aulus was a little baffled until he was able to check with Favorinus, the ultimate authority on every possible subject. When Favorinus contradicted Pliny, Aulus felt secure in accusing the admiral of some extravagance in presentation, but Pliny had long before made provision for protecting himself against people like Aulus Gellius, mere *vititiatores*[12] and quite devoid of true distinction; such persons needed to be reminded that "only phantoms fight with the dead."

Now it is true that Aelian was a miserable scribbler, but Pliny, Seneca, and Plutarch, though sometimes credulous, were not hacks even when it came to science. They were well-read, hard-working, and generally sensible. They sought proof on occasion, and they did not spurn personal observation; on the latter, Pliny, of course, ended up by cutting it a little too fine, but he did not err in principle. Perhaps they read too much or had too much to read without having quite enough information or knowledge to be sufficiently discriminating. Seneca was said to have had research assistants who sometimes led him astray on his facts.[13] There were, however, better scientists than Pliny, Seneca, and Plutarch in these times; as a matter of fact, by comparison with some of the other intellectual activities of the Pax Romana, the work in science is pretty impressive.

Tough, hard-headed old Sextus Julius Frontinus was an author and learned in the law, but he was also an unusually competent civil engineer. Provincial governor, successful general, and respected public servant, Frontinus was asked to solve the problems of the water supply for the city of Rome at a time of life when most men might be ready to retire. The new assignment entailed something more than an excursion into the field of hydrostatics, a branch of knowledge which had attained the status of a real science in the Hellenistic Age and had enjoyed a continuous growth since that time. The Romans had shown considerable aptitude in the practical application of the Greek theoretical advances in this area so that Frontinus presumably had quite a bit to learn about his new job before he could be effective in it. He was already sufficiently prepared to undertake the difficult mathematical computation involved, but there was much special knowledge to be acquired. Frontinus plunged into the water problem and managed to keep afloat. He set out to learn about the construction, length, and capacity of all the aqueducts; in a painstaking survey, plans were drawn and careful analyses made. By new construction, judicious repairs, and by detecting and putting a stop to the illegal diversion of water used in a clandestine way to supply fields, shops, private dwellings, and disorderly houses, Frontinus was able to double the water supply of Rome; more than fifty million gallons a day were henceforth brought into the city. Frontinus was proud of his achievement, and justly so, as anyone who reads his book must readily agree. The younger Pliny greatly admired Frontinus, but they were worlds apart. In a Catonian gesture, the gruff old general refused to countenance any expenditure of funds on a monument to himself. His memory, he said, would endure if his deeds deserved it. Pliny was shocked!

In this era of water-powered mills[14] and piggy-back aqueducts, water was being put to a number of uses. The Archimedean screw for raising water from one level to another was already old hat, and even before the time of Archimedes a talented barber named Ctesibius had invented a pump, a water organ, and a fancy klepsydra. Progress, however, had been made in more recent times. A ground, conical stop-cock for use as a water tap was invented near the beginning of the Christian era.[15] There were horizontal toothed water wheels, vertical geared wheels, and overshot wheels; at a site in Gaul a flour mill was operated with twin sets of eight overshot wheels arranged in series.[16]

In the second half of the first century A.D., there flourished a rather talented fellow named Heron of Alexandria who wrote on mathematics, surveying, pneumatics, automata, and engines of war. Heron was fully acquainted with the work of his predecessors, but he was also a skillful mechanic who was able to improve on some of the older machines and to make new ones of his own. He described a crank-operated apparatus with four toothed wheels which required a force of only five talents to lift a weight of one thousand. Heron also improved upon the water organ, constructed a two-cylinder water pump for use as a fire engine, produced a silf-filling, self trimming oil lamp, a syringe, a screw cutter, a new kind of cupping instrument for surgical use, and various interesting gadgets for the use of priests and magicians.[17] In this final category were altars which, when their fires were lighted, would automatically open temple doors; there were all kinds of singing mechanical birds and self-blowing trumpets operated by water pressure or compressed air. The *Pneumatics* abounds with trick vessels in which liquids remain at a constant level no matter how much is drawn off, jars that produce water or wine, hot or cold water, or fixed amounts of liquid as desired. Many varieties of water clocks are described. The real triumph, however, was a coin-operated sacrificial vessel designed to vend holy water or other liquids when a worshipper dropped a five drachma piece into a slot in the top.[18]

Heron's description of a machine operated by steam — a ball rotated by escaping steam, to be exact — has led some to refer to him as the "father of the turbine." There is some dispute, however, over the originality of Heron's work. It has been contended that he owed much to Ctesibius, Philo, and Strato, but he apparently did make the machines which he describes, and he is conceded to have been a mathematician of no small ability.[19]

The mechanical ingenuity, inventiveness, and gadgeteering of these ancients has been over-emphasized by some modern enthusiasts and disparaged by other writers who are either skeptical or more impressed by the achievements of our own times. On both sides there has been some misrepresentation. The Hellenistic Greeks and the Romans were proficient in mechanics. The engines of Archimedes are for the most part credible enough, and the machines of Heron worked. The greatest failing of antiquity was in a lack of interest in discovering and developing adequate sources of power.

The literature of the Pax Romana hints at many kinds of novelties, mechanical and otherwise, and it will do no real harm to mention a few of them. Despite the skepticism of Aulus Gellius, Favorinus was forced

to admit that the famous dove of Archytas, operated by compressed
air, did indeed fly. Favorinus was patronizing about it, however, and
remarked that once the dove landed it did not rise again. This sort of
disdain calls to mind the story of the chess-playing beagle that was not
a consistent winner. Suetonius has a tale about an inventor who failed
to secure the adoption of a labor-saving device for transporting heavy
columns; the emperor refused to consider using a machine that would
promote unemployment. The nature of the device in question is not
clear, but that such a thing was possible is suggested by a sculptured
relief which shows a huge derrick powered by half a dozen small boys
in a squirrel cage treadmill.[20] The work of Vitruvius abounds in
descriptions of machines for both peace and war; Heron also wrote on
the latter subject. Both Vitruvius and Heron also provide plans for the
construction of hodometers.

On the non-mechanical side we hear of overstuffed sponge uphol-
stery designed to make banqueteers more amorous or fire-proof
garments made from a sort of asbestos linen as well as the use of alum
for fire-proofing wood. A real novelty was a parchment manuscript of
the *Iliad* so minute that it could be enclosed in a nutshell. Much more
important is the revelation of Vitruvius that architects not only drafted
floor plans for projected structures but also drew the elevations. Pliny
mentions illustrated books that showed plants more or less in their true
colors.

Two venerable studies, optics and acoustics, continued to flourish
under the Pax Romana. The remarkable sections on acoustics in the
fifth book of Vitruvius are well known. The wave theory was used to
explain the transmission of sound. It appears in Vitruvius, and Diogenes
Laertius says that a concussion sets up a vibration of sound waves
which move outward spherically from the point of disturbance — he
uses the analogy of the circular motion produced by a stone striking the
water. Pliny was able to demonstrate to his own satisfaction that light
travels faster than sound; he used the example of thunder and lightning,
but no concept of light waves was ever evolved in antiquity.[21]

Perspective, reflection, and refraction were studied by Heron and
Claudius Ptolemy. A very practical application of optics was the
construction of burning mirrors, a complex of mirrors that concen-
trated the rays of the sun on a single point. Archimedes had perhaps
been the first to fashion a burning mirror for military purposes, but
Heron knew all about such things, and his knowledge was passed on to
Anthemius of Tralles, Justinian's architect who helped to rebuild Hagia
Sophia. A hostile, but non-military use of mirrors was ascribed by
Seneca to a certain Hostius. The trick mirrors which so offended Seneca

were no novelty; Aulus Gellius was interested in them and also mentioned the use of the magnifying glass.

Claudius Ptolemy's studies of atmospheric refraction show that the science of optics was employed to provide supplementary proofs for the rotundity of the earth. Actually, there were many simpler types of observation which had already led to this conclusion regarding the shape of our planet. Among seafaring men the common experience of seeing the land rise above or fall beneath the horizon was evidence enough that the earth was a sphere; Aristotle had reasoned the matter out and come to the conclusion that a spherical form was the only one suitable for a body in space; and, as the grammarians pointed out, if the earth was not round, why was it called an orb? Pliny collected these facts and opinions in his *Natural History,* while Diogenes Laertius presented the Stoic and Epicurean views in his *Lives of the Philosophers.* Educated people also knew that the earth rotated on its axis, and they understood fairly well the theory of the precession of the equinoxes. Favorinus, however, like Homer, might occasionally nod: he once explained that the points of the compass are not constant because the sun does not always rise in the same place.

Nevertheless, in the general harmony of belief, there were two areas of disagreement: one concerned the size of the earth, and the other the position of our planet in relation to the rest of the universe.

Pliny was inclined to accept the computation of Eratosthenes which set the circumference of the earth at 252,000 stades, or 31,500 Roman miles. Pliny's source may have Cleomedes who gave the same figure, but Cleomedes also reported the calculation made by Poseidonius who had come up with an estimate of 240,000 stades. Strabo, however, quoted the Poseidonian figure as 180,000, and this was the estimate used by Ptolemy as the basis for his geography. As a result, Columbus and other trusting souls were seriously misled a few centuries later.

The method of Poseidonius and Eratosthenes was perfectly sound. They chose two points on the surface of the globe that lay on one of the great circles. After measuring the distance between the two points, they observed the difference in elevation of a given star at these points and so calculated the ratio of the arc to the great circle. Eratosthenes chose the sun as his star and Syene and Alexandria as his two points; he found the arc to be one-fiftieth of the circle, the distance between the two towns he thought to be 5000 stades, and therefore the circumference of the earth must be fifty times the distance between Syene and Alexandria. Poseidonius chose Alexandria and Rhodes, measured the distance between them as 5000 stades, used Canopus as his star, and calculated his arc as one forty-eighth of a great circle. As it turned out, both men made errors in measurement, but some of the errors offset others; thus the results were, all things considered, reasonably good.

The circumferences of 250,000 and 240,000 stades reported by Cleomedes as the calculations of Eratosthenes and Poseidonius respectively seems plausible enough, but the 180,000 stades mentioned by Strabo and used by Ptolemy does pose a problem. It may be, however, that the difference between 240,000 and 180,000 stades is more apparent than real because of the varying length of the stade at one time or another.[22] Apparently, people just refused to call a stade a stade.

On the question of the heliocentric or geocentric universe opinion was becoming pretty one-sided by the Roman imperial era. Aristarchus had proposed his heliocentric theory in the third century B.C., but it had failed to gain general acceptance. Some people simply could not reconcile themselves to the idea of living on a satellite; others refused to allow this new-fangled notion to conflict with their religious beliefs; and the astronomers could not harmonize the concept with certain seemingly workable hypotheses for other phenomena. Pliny was convinced by "irrefragable arguments" of geocentricity,[23] while Ptolemy, who really understood the arguments, agreed with him. The earth, said Ptolemy, was at the center of the heavens, the earth and the universe were spherical in form, and that was that.

The authority of Ptolemy, soon perceived and long accepted, was certainly well deserved even if only on a relative basis. A giant among pygmies, he lived in, but was not part of, the Second Age of the Sophists. As energetic and tireless as the elder Pliny, he far surpassed the amiable admiral in ability. Like everyone else in this period, Ptolemy read and used the work of his predecessors, but he was no jackdaw content to adorn his nest with borrowed finery; instead, he contributed something new to almost every subject with which he concerned himself. The *Almagest* is an overwhelming treatise with its calculations, tables, and hypotheses relating to astronomical phenomena: the earth, sun, moon, fixed stars, and the five visible planets. In this greatest of all astronomical works of classical antiquity, Ptolemy surpassed even the great Hipparchus whom he modestly called his master.

Although Ptolemy also wrote on music and chronology and did important work in optics, his most influential book next to the *Almagest* was the *Geography*. In the Roman imperial period Strabo, Pomponius Mela, and Pliny had attempted to describe the inhabited world. Of the three, Strabo was the most successful, but he was no scientist, and his descriptive geography could be no better than the sources which he employed for information about areas outside the Roman Empire. Strabo was what Ptolemy would call a chorographer, while Ptolemy himself was a mathematical geographer in the tradition of Eratosthenes and Hipparchus; the objectives of Strabo and Ptolemy were not the same, and thus there is no basis for ranking the two on a comparative scale. Ptolemy's interest in geography was cartographic. He wished to determine the latitudes and longitudes of regions and places in order to represent them on a series of maps. Ptolemy based his work on that of Marinus of Tyre. He corrected what he believed to be the errors of Marinus and added new material which had come to light. His statement that it is important to pay attention to new records[24] epitomizes his whole attitude toward research; his was a novel point of view in an age of academic bee eaters. In the mass, the geographical gazetteer that Ptolemy turned out was impressive, too, though not to the same extent as the *Almagest*. Like other scientists of antiquity, his fault was not so much one of calculation or method as of measurement. He simply did not have the basic data that were necessary for his project.

In contrast to the methods and achievements of a Ptolemy or a Heron or a Frontinus, we may glance for a moment at the modes of arriving at an explanation for certain natural phenomena: comets, thunder, lightning, volcanic eruptions, and earthquakes. In general, an educated man tended to adopt the explanation provided by the particular philosophic system which he had espoused. Sometimes these explanations were similar or identical in the various systems; often, they might be quite different. The Epicureans, for example, believed the universe to be infinite in extent, whereas the Stoics thought it was finite. The Epicureans went against prevailing opinion in maintaining that a world need not be spherical in shape since some worlds might be oval or formed into other non-spherical shapes. The Stoics and Epicureans both thought that our world would come to an end, but for different reasons. Seneca[25] expected a great deluge that would destroy man and all his works and usher in a new age, but some others a little more abreast of the news must have felt that Seneca was a little behind the times.

Many of the explanations provided by the philosophic systems had been adopted by their founders who in turn borrowed from earlier scientist-philosophers. This meant in some cases that the hypotheses were old fashioned, dating from the fourth century or earlier, and had not been revised to take into account even the discoveries of the Hellenistic Age. This was not true in every instance, but the common tendency, even where more recent speculation might be known to the writers of the Pax Romana, was to follow the party line.

The frequency of earthquakes in classical lands very naturally promoted much interest in this dreadful phenomenon. Records of severe earthquakes were gathered by the historians: Strabo refers to Democles of Phrygia and Demetrius of Callatis as compiling catalogues of famous earthquakes, and Seneca adds Theophrastus to his list of authorities. The various types of shocks and their effects were carefully described by the scientists. In addition, there was much theorizing about the cause of earthquake.

Diodorus says that the Egyptians predicted earthquakes by studying the stars; he adds that the Babylonians foretold these calamities from an observation of the rising, setting, and color of the planets. Pliny said that the Babylonians thought earthquakes were caused by "the force of the stars." The Assyrian evidence does not support Pliny's statement. It seems clear that the Assyrians attributed earthquakes to Ea, the god of the underground waters;[26] moreover, they were much more concerned with the phenomenon as an omen and what it might portend if it occurred in a particular month.[27] The Sumerian word for earthquake was *nun-gal*; this was also the name of an underworld deity,[28] and this suggests that earthquakes were attributed by the Sumerians to this god rather than to the stars or some heavenly deity.

The early Greeks and the uneducated people of the later classical period were content to blame some god or evil spirit when an earthquake occurred. From Homer onward, the sea god Poseidon was called the Earth Shaker. Herodotus reported a Thessalian belief that the Vale of Tempe was the handiwork of Poseidon; he agreed that it must have been the consequence of an earthquake. Other authors in addition to Herodotus dealt with the land changes that might result from earthquakes: Aristotle, Lucretius, Strabo, Seneca, Pliny, and Ammianus Marcellinus.

Various types of earthquakes were distinguished. Aristotle[29] mentioned horizontal and vertical shocks; Pliny spoke of (1) a quiver and swell and (2) a waving bend;[30] Seneca quoted Poseidonius as describing a kind called succession, when the earth moved up and down, and another sort called inclination, when the earth was shaken and sloped to one side like a boat;[31] Seneca himself thought he could distinguish a third, a darting and pushing forward. Ammianus listed four varieties: *brasmatiae* (upheaving), *chasmatiae* (gaping), *climatiae* (inclination), and *mycematiae* which were heard with a "threatening roar as the elements break up."[32] The Epicureans spoke of tremblings, openings, and lateral and vertical displacements.[33]

The sixth book of Seneca's *Natural Questions* is concerned with earthquakes. Seneca was a Stoic and also fancied himself as a scholar. Committed to the Stoic explanation, he nevertheless put on a show of learning by listing the various theories about the cause of earthquake which had been advanced in the past. Thales, of course, chose water as his cause: the earth was like a boat floating on the surface of the ocean, and it tipped when the water was rough. Anaximenes thought that the earth itself was the chief cause. Aristotle quoted Anaximenes as saying that the earth broke when in the process of becoming wet or dry which explained why earthquakes occurred during droughts or heavy rains. Anaxagoras, according to Seneca, believed that fire was responsible: it heated the internal waters to the boiling point. Somebody was wrong about this, however, because both Aristotle and Ammianus quoted Anaxagoras as saying that air was the cause, since "air, whose natural motion is upwards, causes earthquakes when it is trapped in hollows beneath the earth, which happens when the upper parts of the earth get clogged by rain...." Democritus combined wind and water in his explanation, according to Seneca, whereas Aristotle understood Democritus to say that rain water in excess would fill the cavities of the earth and cause trouble as it tried to escape, or else the drying up of the earth would draw water from one place to another underground.

Archelaus and Aristotle had settled on wind as the disturbing agent. Wind, said Aristotle, had the greatest motive power; it was the substance most violent in action with the greatest velocity, and it also possessed the most prolonged motion and the finest penetration. This wind theory became the most widely accepted. It was adopted by the Peripatetics, Stoics, and Epicureans. Theophrastus, Strabo, Lucretius, and Seneca all subscribed to it, and Pliny merely said: "I think it indubitable that their [the earthquakes'] cause is to be attributed to the winds."

Diogenes Laertius quoted Poseidonius as representing the Stoic version that earthquakes occurred when the wind was imprisoned or found its way into the hollow parts of the earth. Seneca sneered that the Epicureans could find no more certain cause of earthquake than the wind. He himself came to the conclusion that the earth was shaken when the wind had engulfed itself in the cavities of the earth and was trying to escape.

The Epicurean point of view was summarized by Diogenes Laertius by quoting the letter of Epicurus to Pythocles. There was also the fuller version in Lucretius in which four causes were enumerated: (1) the collapse of the roof and sides of a subterranean cavern which might spread a tremor over the earth; (2) earth dislodged might fall into a subterranean lake and the agitation of the water communicated to the earth itself; (3) wind gathering in the hollows would buffet the caverns and cause the earth to lean in that direction; and (4) wind coming from without or rising in the earth might burst out with violence. In the latter instance only would the wind actually be a direct agent in causing earthquake.

Seneca made it perfectly clear that no earthquake should be thought to have been caused by the gods, but not everyone approached the subject in this rational way. Aulus Gellius[34] was not at all sure that the natural philosophers with their causes of wind or water were getting at the truth. It was disturbing that they did not agree; it was by no means certain that the gods should be ruled out. Cicero[35] put earthquakes in the category of portents as did Pliny and others. The coming of an earthquake could be predicted by sailors, or by observing the weather and the behaviour of animals, reptiles, and insects.[36]

As the centuries passed, the frontiers of science retreated rather than advanced. Typical of Christian science was the attitude of the Venerable Bede who attributed earthquakes to a sea beast which lay in the ocean wrapped around the world and holding its tail in its mouth. When scorched by the sun this creature struggled so mightily that it shook the earth.[37] Thus, in the thirteen centuries between Thales and Bede, the ancient world had completed the circle of its thought and dived again into the primeval waters in search of an explanation.

Sextus Empiricus, who was against practically everything, attacked (among others) and destroyed (to his own satisfaction) the geometer and arithmeticians. His sortie against the geometers was not very impressive, nor can the assault on the arithmeticians have influenced many people who had already made up their minds one way or another. The geometers were well entrenched. They had something to show for their efforts; it was a little hard to convince anyone that Archimedes, Eratosthenes, Heron, or Ptolemy had labored in vain.

With the arithmeticians, on the other hand, the case was different. Their stock in trade was not arithmetic. *That* was called logistics, and no one doubted its usefulness. But *arithmetike* dealt with number. It was a pseudo-science with some application in the field called music, but its founder had been Pythagoras. This worthy and his disciples had carried or dragged number to a distance that was positively indecent. Sextus was certainly not the first person to feel that the idea of the "tetrakys" was preposterous. The tetrakys was the sum of 1, 2, 3, and 4. The world-shaking thing about it was that "one" determined a point; "two," a line; "three," a plane; and "four" a solid. This made "ten" very significant and basic number which somehow had something to d with the fact that people had ten fingers and ten toes and used the decimal system. A clever man might even be able to find the appropriate numbers for the soul or the universe. Plato had been taken in by this fiddle-faddle, a circumstance that did not endanger its perpetuation.

At the beginning of the second century A.D. *arithmetike* was generally the property of the Neo-Pythagoreans. The great miracle worker, Apollonius of Tyana, more or less belonged to this sect although there were Neo-Pythagoreans more conservative and less flamboyant than he. A treatise on *arithmetike* by Nicomachus of Gerasa[38] has survived. It contains the usual tripe, and it would be a great stroke of business if some way could be found to exchange it for any one of the dozens of books written in the second century which are not now extant. Even one of the effusions of Favorinus would be more welcome than the numerical labyrinth of Nichomachus.

Sextus Empiricus also went a round with the astrologers, or exponents of the "mathematical art." Astrology, said Sextus, was not to be confused with astronomy. He admitted that others had attacked the astrologers, but said that he would fight at close range. Some people had already denied the claim of the astrologers that "terrestrial" things "sympathized" with "celestial" ones. Another old argument was that since all events did not occur because of destiny, but sometimes through chance, necessity, or personal decisions, the astrologers could not possibly predict all things.[39] Sextus contented himself with proving the absurdity of the horoscope, and, as usual, he was certain of his triumph.

While the Neo-Pythagoreans had made a number of converts in the era of the Good Emperors, the astrologers were even more flourishing.[40] The most eminent scientist of the age, a man who had proved his worth in mathematics, astronomy, and geography, was a firm believer in astrology. He was not only a believer, but he also became an authority on the subject by writing about it. The name of the book was the *Tetrabiblos*; the name of the author, Claudius Ptolemy.

Ptolemy's argument was that the sun and moon and their movements obviously affected physical conditions on the earth, and therefore it was logical to believe that the heavenly bodies could affect other terrestrial matters as well. There were all kinds of variables, of course. It was difficult to make astrology into an exact science because the whole matter was so complicated. There was one set of rules governing individuals and another for making predictions about regions or nations. Nevertheless, prognostication could be very useful: if a person knew what to expect, he could prepare for it. It was just like getting ready for winter.

With its chariots, thrones, houses, faces, and so on, astrology was no picnic. Just as with any science, there was a special terminology or jargon. Ptolemy started out with the simple aspects and went on to the more advanced concepts. It was important, for example, to know the powers of the planets. The effect of the sun was heating and drying, while the moon had a humidifying influence because of its proximity to the earth. Saturn cooled and dried because it was so far away, but Jupiter was hot and humid. The beneficent planets were Jupiter, Venus, and the moon; the reverse was true of Saturn and Mars. The planets possessed gender: the moon and Venus were female; Saturn, Jupiter, and Mars were male, of course, but poor Mercury was neuter. It was a crowning mercy that stars changed their gender as they preceded or followed the sun. The seasons and the four points of the compass all had differing properties. Putting all these things together in order to make a prognostication was a messy business to say the least.

National characteristics were predetermined by the terrestrial location and celestial affiliations of the peoples concerned. In the northwest corner of the inhabited world nations were affected by Aries and Mars; this made the Gauls, Britons, and Germans fierce, headstrong, and bestial. Nations in the east were affected by the sun and were therefore naturally right-handed; the moon affected those in the west to make them soft and secretive. All kinds of predictions were possible: the weather, military events, birth, length of life, the sex of an unborn child, and individual temperament. The horoscopes which Ptolemy draws are almost identical with those which can still be found in some of our daily newspapers. Our astrologers are probably not as proficient as Ptolemy, but their prophecies enjoy a wider circulation.

But there is yet another link between the Pax Romana and the uncertain peace of our times. Lucian in his lighter moods was a classical Jules Verne who envisioned interplanetary travel in the *Icaromenippus* and added the untruth of space warfare to the *True History*. As Seneca predicted, "These things which are now hidden shall be discovered by time and the diligence of future ages. Many things are reserved for the generations to come when our memory shall be extinguished. The world is a little thing...."[41]

FOOTNOTES

1. Apuleius, *Apology*, 29-30 and 40.
2. Lucian, *Dipsas*, 3.
3. Aulus Gellius, *Attic Nights*, VII, 3; Pliny, *Natural History*, VIII,

4. Philostratus, *Life of Apollonius*, III, 49.

5. Lucian, *Icaromenippus*.

6. Pausanias, *Description of Greece*, IX, 20, 4.

7. Plutarch, *Cleverness of Animals*.

8. Pliny, *Natural History*, IX, 8; Pliny the Younger, *Letters*, IX, 33; Plutarch, *Cleverness of Animals*, 984; Aulus Gellius, *Attic Nights*, VI, 8; Aelian, *Characteristics of Animals*, VI, 15.

9. *Attic Nights*, V, 2; Pliny, *Natural History*, VIII, 63; Plutarch, *op. cit.* 970.

10. *Attic Nights*, V, 14; Pliny, *op. cit.*, VIII, 21; Aelian, *op. cit.*, VII, 48.

11. *Attic Nights*, IX, 4 and X, 12.

12. Pliny, *Natural History*, Preface 30-33.

13. Quintilian, *Institutes*, X, 1, 128.

14. Vitruvius, *Architecture*, X, 12.

15. A. G. Drachmann, "Ktesibius, Philon, and Heron," *Acta Historica Scientiorum Naturalium et Medicinalum* (Copenhagen), Vol. IV (1948), preface.

16. C. Singer, *History of Technology*, Oxford 1956, Vol. II, pp. 595-597; see also F. C. Moore, "Three Canal Projects," *American Journal of Archaeology*, 44 (1950), pp. 97-111.

17. Drachmann, *op. cit.*, pp. 92-157; B. Woodcroft, *Pneumatics of Heron of Alexandria*, London 1851.

18. Woodcroft, *op. cit.*, p. 21.

19. Ivor Thomas, *Greek Mathematical Works*, Cambridge 1941, Vol. I, pp. 466-509.

20. Singer, *op. cit.*, Vol. II, pp. 660-661; illustrated in C. Herschel, *Frontinus and the Water Supply of the City of Rome*, New York 1913, p. 247.

21. S. Sambursky, "On some References to Experience in Stoic Physics," *Isis*, 49 (1958), pp. 331-335.

22. I. E. Drabkin, "Poseidonius and the Circumference of the Earth," *Isis*, 34 (1943), pp. 509-512; A. Diller, "Ancient Measurements of the Earth," *Isis*, 40 (1949), pp. 6-9.

23. Pliny, *Natural History*, II, 69.

24. Ptolemy, *Almagest*, I, 1.

25. Seneca, *Natural Questions*, III, 29-30.

26. L. Waterman, *Royal Correspondence of the Assyrian Empire* (4 vols. Ann Arbor 1930), Vol. I, nos. 191, 355, 357.

27. R. C. Thompson, *Reports of the Magicians and Astrologers of Nineveh and Babylon* (2 vols. London 1900), Vol. II, pp. lxxxi-lxxxiv.

28. A. Deimel, *Akkadisch-Sumerisches Glossar*, Rome 1937, p. 392.

29. Aristotle, *Meteorologica*, II, 8.

30. Pliny, *Natural History*, II, 84.

31. Seneca, *Natural Questions*, VI, 21.

32. Ammianus, XVII, 7, 13-14.

33. Diogenes Laertius, *Lives of the Philosophers*, VII, 157.

34. Aulus Gellius, *Attic Nights*, II, 28.

35. Cicero, *De Divinatione*, 35.

36. Pliny, *Natural History*, II, 83 and 86; Aelian, *op. cit.*, VI, 16 and IX, 19.

37. F. D. Adams, *Birth and Development of the Geological Sciences*, Baltimore 1938, pp. 403-404.

38. M. L. D'Ooge, *Nichomachus of Gerasa*, New York 1926.

39. Sextus Empiricus, *Against the Astrologers*, V, 44 and 46-48.

40. F. H. Cramer, *Astrology in Roman Law and Politics*, Philadelphia 1954.

41. Seneca, *Natural Questions*, VII, 25 and 31.

The Labyrinth

This is the Ennead that came forth from the unoriginated Father who alone himself is Father and Mother whose fullness encompasses the Twelve Deeps.

Coptic Gnostic Treatise

Avoid the noxious weeds that grow where Jesus Christ does not cultivate the soil.

St. Ignatius to the Philadelphians

With respect to the great multitude of believers, it were better for them to believe without a reason.

Origen

IN THE SECOND CENTURY A.D. the intellectual life of the Greco-Roman world reached something more than an impasse. It wound up in a gigantic log jam that remained unbroken until blown to bits by Christian dynamite.

It is unnecessary to debate the merits of Christianity as a religion in order to appreciate its salutary effect upon intellectual activity in the ancient world. The new faith was sufficiently novel in its combination of older elements to stimulate study and speculation. It gave those who wanted to think something different to think about. A new frontier of scholarship challenged the ambitious; fresh subjects invited the application of traditional methods of research, while the missionaries from Judaea introduced techniques of the synagogue that were previously unfamiliar to the Gentiles.

This was not the first time, nor the last, that cultural self-asphyxiation was to be arrested by the drafts of diffusion. In the Hellenistic age, contact with the Greeks had revived thought in the Near East: it did something for Zoroastrianism, and it enlivened Judaism, some felt, to a point of over-stimulation. In the second and third centuries A.D., when crossed with Greco-Roman elements, Christianity itself was to bear some of the strange fruits of Gnosticism.

The religion of the Christians was a century old before its adherents began variously to battle or to join forces with the high intellectual

tradition of classical antiquity. The earliest preaching, that of the
Apostolic Age, had concerned itself almost entirely with two matters
the elucidation of the prophetic message of the Old Testament in
support of the view that Jesus was the Messiah, and the perpetuation o
the "living memory" of the Saviour as preserved in the recollections o
the Apostles and the orally transmitted *Logia*. Later, the Synoptic
Gospels were written to immortalize and consolidate the oral tradition
and, along with the Gospels, the Apostolic letters came to be treasured
by the churches. Near the end of the first century A.D., a new phase
commenced with the writings of the Apostolic Fathers: the letters o
Clement, Ignatius, Polycarp, for example, as well as the *Shepherd o
Hermas*, the *Didache* (Teaching of the Apostles), and so on. It has been
remarked that these latter epistles and didactic compositions were
characterized by literary simplicity, earnest religious conviction, an
freedom from Hellenic philosophy and rhetoric, although Jaeger's fin
analysis of the first letter of Clement has demonstrated the presence o
strong and hitherto unsuspected rhetorical influence.[1]

By the reign of Hadrian, some of the growing Christian literature
began to be addressed to an audience wider than that represented b
the local congregations. To explain the faith to prospective convert
and to defend it against the slanders of pagan attackers, the "apology
was introduced. The letters, acts *(praxeis)*, sermons *(diatribes)*, an
didactic works previously employed by the Christians were common
enough literary forms in the ancient world, but the apology was the
most conscious rhetorical device used in Christian literature up to the
middle of the second century A.D. A landmark in the process of the
Hellenization of Christianity, a process which accelerated rapidly after
150, apologetic writing was soon joined by other forms of composition
that were increasingly "Hellenic" in rhetorical style and philosophical
content.

Against the prevailing opinion that the Christians tried to approac
the educated pagans by adopting forms familiar to the latter, a
subsequently by using Greek philosophy as common ground on whic
to meet, one must protest that this is putting the cart before the horse
It was not the Hellenization of Christianity that Christianized the
"Greeks," but rather the Christianization of the Greeks that Hellenize
Christianity. In other words, people who had become Christian
naturally applied to the propagation and study of the new faith the
training they had received in the pagan schools. This trend wa
particularly apparent in the period between Justin Martyr in the
mid-second century and the *floruit* of Origen in the third. By the latte
date, a system of *Christian* education was beginning to evolve. By the

education, though adopting much that was traditional, was being adapted to peculiar Christian needs; the tool was subordinated to the material for which it was employed, whereas in the preceding half-century or so the tool had been used on the material experimentally. At any rate, the Hellenization of Christianity was symptomatic of the spread of the faith, an index of its acceptance by the intelligentsia.

The engagement and ultimate wedding of Christianity and Hellenism was not equally pleasing to all the relatives of the happy couple. On both sides, pagan and Christian, protests were to be heard for some time. To cite only two extreme and well known examples: Porphyry, the Neo-platonist, felt that Origen, recognized as a brilliant student of philosophy, had taken the wrong turning, while the polemical Christian, Tatian, could find little to admire in the "Greeks." Greek philosophy seemed an idle, even a dangerous and subversive, thing to many churchmen; in addition, the traditional pagan system of education was subjected to some very acute criticism. One of the system's greatest defects was identified by Justin who condemned its excessive reverence for the past and recommended, "We should scorn to follow the opinions of the ancients if they are worthless." Tatian, like some of the pagans themselves, sneered at the grammarians who "used builder's tools without knowing how to build." These same grammarians, along with teachers of more elevated status, all promised vainly "to make their disciples happy"; these were the words of Athenagoras, who must have heard lectures in the style of those preserved for us in the *Grammatici Graeci*. Rhetoric and sophistry were obvious targets: "skill in oratory rather than proof by deeds"; or "an attitude towards even the clearest truth is affected by the orator's talents and the power of his eloquence," or again, "the art of sophistry is a fantastic power which makes false opinions like true by means of words." The "Greeks" were also addicted to plagiarism, said Clement of Alexandria, and very soon Hippolytus proved that not even Christians were immune to this disease, for, in refuting all heresies, the good Bishop of Portus refuted most of them with the help of generous and unacknowledged extracts from Sextus Empiricus. Origen, like Galen, was contemptuous of the way in which a man became attached to a particular school of philosophy; it was irrational because it happened either by chance, "or because he is provided with a teacher of that school," or through *belief,* rather than knowledge afforded by study, that one sect was superior to another.

Grammar, rhetoric, oratory, and philosophy, the principal branches of pagan education, were thus brought under fire, but the more specialized interests of the pagans were generally ignored. Tatian, of course, was an exception: his attitude toward medicine was that of a proto-Christian-Scientist, and he also said, "How can I believe one who tells me that the sun is a red-hot mass and the moon an earth?" Hippolytus, aided by Sextus Empiricus, attacked the astrologers and arithmeticians, but his attitude toward saner studies was not so fierce. "This Ptolemy," he said, "does not seem to me to be entirely useless," although he went on to point out that Ptolemy's obvious talents had been expended on matters of no real consequence.

In the end, however, one can only conclude that the aims rather than the methods of the pagans offended the Christians since techniques identical with those of the pagans were employed for Christian activities. There was the appeal to authority, first to the Old and then later to the New Testament as well as to the church authors. Commentary and argumentation were standard procedures. In the *Octavius*, Minucius Felix praised his protagonist for supporting views "by a wealth of argument, examples, and quotations from authorities." And, of course, Minucius used the familiar pagan literary form of the dialogue for his work. Christian commentaries also remind us of the legal literature, as in the following extracts:[2]

> It was, I consider, a violent and unwarranted procedure which was adopted by Heracleon...in discussing this sentence.... For he says.... He deals with the statement with some degree of audacity...we need not waste our time in rebutting.

> The question is raised, whether Samuel rose by the hand of the sorceress or not. And if, indeed, we were to allow that he did rise, we should be propounding what is false....

Even in the interpretation of the Old Testament, the Christians were, largely through Philo, the debtors of the Greeks. That learned Alexandrian had applied to the Old Testament the allegorical method developed by the Greeks for the elucidation of Homer, and his works were familiar to Justin, Athenagoras, Clement of Alexandria, Origen and many others. Interpretation by allegory came into Christian method so early that Eusebius thought Philo's description of the Therapeutae, "who expounded the sacred writings allegorically," actually referred to Philo's Christian contemporaries in Egypt." Clement of Alexandria maintained that the truth was veiled in literature by figures, symbols, and enigmas; in the Old Testament and in Greek literature and philosophy, divine truths might be found by "true philosophy."

It was undoubtedly this same Clement of Alexandria who gave the greatest impetus to the process by means of which "two universal systems, Greek culture and the Christian church, were to be united in the mighty superstructure of Alexandrian theology."[4] Clement (*fl.* 200 A.D.), after receiving a full measure of traditional education including instruction in philosophy, had been converted to Christianity. In Rome he listened to the lectures of Tatian; even if he had failed to tell us that he had heard "the Assyrian," we should be able to recognize his indebtedness, although Tatian failed to convince Clement that "the Greeks" were worthless. Later on, Clement came to Alexandria to sit at the feet of Pantaenus whom he was to succeed as the head of the Catechetical School there. The results were not at all surprising: in Alexandria, the stronghold of Philo, Judaism had become strongly Hellenized, and Alexandrine Christianity was unlikely to escape the same fate, particularly under the guidance of Clement.

Of the ten works of Clement known to Eusebius, we know three: *Exhortation to the Heathen, Paedagogus,* and the *Stromata.* The last was the most extensive and the most revealing. A patch-work, Eusebius called it, the *Stromata* was better organized than the *Attic Nights* of Aulus Gellius or the *Meditations* of Marcus Aurelius, but it was of the same genre. Like Galen, Clement wrote to "aid the weakness of his memory." Lecture notes, notes from reading, and opinions gradually formed over the years filled eight books of which the last was entirely a handbook of dialectic and quite different from any of its predecessors; if Eusebius had not attested the existence of the eighth book, we might be inclined to question it as part of the original, for it seems more like a later addition by some copyist.

Eusebius called the *Stromata* erudite, and, by second or early third century standards, it certainly was in its wealth of quotation from pagan authors ranging all the way from Homer and Hesiod to Dionysius Thrax and Berosus. Almost every one of the forty school authors was either quoted or mentioned along with Moschion, Panyasis, Alexander Polyhistor, Philo, and Josephus. A true Greek, Clement ignored the Latin writers, even Cicero and Virgil. Among the other early Christian authors, only Athenagoras, Justin, and Theophilus showed, or were at pains to show, marked familiarity with the pagan authors, and their display was much less spectacular than Clement's.

For Clement, the purpose and content of education for Christianity was crystal clear:

I am not oblivious of what is babbled by some, who in their ignorance are frightened at every noise, and say that we ought to occupy ourselves with what is most necessary, and which contains the faith; but as a man can be a believer without learning, so also it is impossible for a man without learning to comprehend the things which are declared in the faith."[5]

Knowledge, for Clement as for Plutarch, Quintilian, and Tacitus required nature (natural endowment), reason (instruction), and habit (constant practice). "Many things equip the artist," and "training aid perception, for it is not by nature, but by learning, that people become noble and good, as people also become physicians and pilots."[6] "I call him truly learned who brings everything to bear on the truth; so that from geometry, and music, and grammar, and philosophy itself, culling what is useful, he guards the faith against assault."[7] Philosophy was a necessary preparation for Christianity; God had given it to the Greek (as He had given the Jews the Law) until He should call them. In philosophy, the Christian should be an eclectic, employing what was best from all schools. All in all, the fields of Christianity must be watered with "the liquid streams of Greek learning."

One must begin, however, with Faith. Although Knowledge is founded on demonstration by a process of reasoning, first principles are incapable of demonstration, for they are known neither by art nor sagacity. The first cause must be apprehended by Faith alone. Armed with Faith and Knowledge, the true meaning of the hidden word can be discovered and the ultimate in Christian understanding achieved.

As Origen, the pupil and successor of Clement, explained it, neither the Old nor the New Testament in their entirety could be taken literally. In the *De Principiis,* Origen maintained that "obstacles and impossibilities" had been introduced into the sacred law and history as signs that the obvious (literal) meaning was not the whole of the message. "The Scriptures and Gospels do not contain a pure history of events, but also those which did not occur.... and the law and commandments are sometimes irrational and impossible of literal observance." There is throughout the Scriptures a "spiritual" meaning but the portions which have a "bodily" or literal meaning are limited in number. The spiritual meaning could be learned only through study and the application of the allegorical method. Such advanced activity must be preceded by training; at Alexandria, this meant a liberal education capped by instruction in Greek philosophy.

Origen was a brilliant student who had gone through the traditional curriculum in grammar and rhetoric in addition to receiving a thorough training in the Scriptures; he also studied philosophy with the great teacher Ammonius — who later lapsed from Christianity into paganism (to the delight of Porphyry). At eighteen, Origen, who was making a living as a teacher of literature, began to direct catechetical instruction at Alexandria. He soon abandoned literature, sold his books, and concentrated on teaching philosophy and theology. Like many a modern instructor, he devoted the day to instructing his students and the night to his own research. But Origen was at last more fortunate than most: he appointed one of his best students to teach the undergraduates while he confined himself to seminars and research. He developed a production line for the latter, and, as he turned out his commentaries, he dictated to seven shorthand writers.... "and as many copyists as well as girls skilled in penmanship." Still later, he allowed his public discourses to be taken down in shorthand for publication.

The curriculum at Alexandria under Origen included "the ordinary elementary subjects," geometry, arithmetic, and other preliminary studies followed by an examination of the main systems of philosophy. Gregory Thaumaturgus testified that geometry and astronomy were taught by Origen as preliminaries to philosophy and that the survey of the philosophic systems aimed at the acquisition of an eclecticism for use in theological studies; the main stress, as with Clement, was on dialectic rather than "science" or "ethics" since Christianity had no need of the first and possessed an ethic of its own. Unlike Clement, who lectured, Origen often employed the Socratic method of discussion. The command of philosophy possessed by Origen was admitted even by his enemy, Porphyry, and his brilliance was well calculated to win converts among the intellectuals. Gregory, who had studied oratory and planned to enter the law, was led away to philosophy and theology by Origen.

In addition to his commentaries which, according to Porphyry, "introduced Greek ideas into foreign fables," Origen learned Hebrew so that he might read the Old Testament in the original and compare it with the Greek translations, and he collated the Septuagint with other translations into the Greek which he discovered by a diligent search. The scholarship of Origen suffers by comparison with that of Sextus Julius Africanus, however, if their analysis of the story of Susanna is any criterion. Africanus objected to this passage in the Septuagint Book of Daniel on the grounds (a) that it was not found in the Hebrew, (b) that Daniel was made to prophesy by inspiration rather than in his usual way by visions, dreams, or angelic visitations, and (c) that the Greek text depended for its effect upon puns which would have no meaning in Hebrew. Thus, he reasoned, the passage must be a modern forgery. Origen's reply was learned, if not completely to the point, and full of many examples from his work on the collation of the

Septuagint. He argued that, although the Susanna story was not found in the Hebrew, it did appear in several of the Greek translations other than the Septuagint. The apparent explanation was therefore that the Jews had later excised the tale because of their policy of hiding from the people "scandalous stories" that would discredit elders, rulers, or judges. Daniel *must* have been like the other prophets since *they* prophesied by inspiration. Africanus was chided as irreverent even to suggest that the passage was not genuine, nor could Origen agree that the style was different. Furthermore, the story of Susanna was full of exquisite thoughts which lent themselves to instructive exposition, and thus it could not be spurious.

The trouble with the allegorical method was that it could not be controlled. It was not quite the same as working out a mathematical problem for which there was only one correct answer about which there could be no dispute. Clement and Origen skated on the edges of orthodoxy where the ice was thin. Moreover, long before them the dangerous mingling of Greek philosophy with amorphous Christian theology had encouraged heresy to raise its hydra-headed menace. Tertullian and his predecessors were quick to blame philosophy: the Valentinians had read too much of Plato; Marcion had been corrupted by Stoicism; the dialectic of Aristotle had been the ruin of many a Christian. Porphyry, of course, claimed that the Christians had misused philosophy.

Among the early Christian polemicists, Tatian had not stopped with the castigation of philosophy, for he had roundly condemned everything Greek. Whatever the Greeks had, they had stolen it from the barbarians. By his chronological calculations, Tatian proved that Moses was earlier than Homer and the principal source of Greek wisdom; subsequent Christian writers availed themselves of Tatian's research and borrowed his arguments. A hearer of Justin and a great champion against the pagans, Tatian nevertheless ended his days a heretic. He was better at tearing down than at building up. His *Diatessaron* combined the four gospels into a single work by weaving the accounts together in a way that reduced the total number of verses by about one-fourth; it is revealing of Tatian's attitude that, by eliminating duplications and matters of which he did not approve, he retained only half of Mark, two-thirds of Luke, three-fourths of Matthew, and virtually all of John!

Although many churchmen composed tracts against the multitude of heresies that appeared in the second and third centuries, those of the West were most positive in their answer to heresy. They adopted a uniform stand, whereas their counterparts in the East tended to be more individualistic. Irenaeus, Tertullian, and others found their solution in tradition and authority. The teaching of the Church, they said, was everywhere and always the same; it was based on the witness of the prophets, the apostles, and all the disciples. Athens and Jerusalem, the Academy and the Church, heretics and Christians, Tertullian proclaimed, had nothing in common. "We have no need of curiosity after Jesus Christ, nor of research after the Gospels." The yardstick was the rule of faith as expressed in the Creed, such a rule encouraged questions only among heretics. This much the Christians owed to the law of Rome. Yet Tertullian, another great champion, died a Montanist!

Many heresies were characterized as Gnostic. Most churchmen felt that Gnosticism had arisen through the introduction of philosophy into Christianity; Porphyry, on the contrary, said that it had resulted from the introduction of Christianity into philosophy. In recent times, it has been argued that Gnosticism had its origin in Jewish apocalyptic thought during the first two Christian centuries.[8] Perhaps, however, the newly discovered Chenoboskion documents when fully studied will give a more positive answer.[9] It does, at the moment, seem quite possible that there were Gnostics who were never Christians, nor Jews, nor "Greeks." One suspects also that Gnostic is too broad a category, for Clement of Alexandria thought *he* was a Gnostic.

Wisdom, said Clement, is certain knowledge *(gnosis)*, a sure apprehension of things divine and human; it comprehends the present, past, and future, and it is irrefragable by reason inasmuch as it has been communicated. Philosophers copy the truth after the manner of painting, and the Law is only the shadow of Truth, but gnosis is that which has descended by transmission to the few: the Gnostics are the elite.

The Gnostic must be erudite. Gnosis is essentially a contemplation of existences on the part of the soul; it is an attribute of the rational soul which trains itself by knowledge so that it may become entitled to immortality. The (Christian) Gnostic must become like Christ, his Teacher, in the complete eradication of desire which reaps as its fruit impassibility. Gnosis is not born with men, but is acquired, and this necessitates application, training, and progress. Man was not perfect in his creation but adapted to the reception of virtue. The Gnostic always occupies himself with the things of highest importance, but if he does have leisure, he applies himself to philosophy which is for him the dessert after the main meal. In disease, accident, and death, the Gnostic remains inflexible, for he knows that these are the necessities of creation. He is moral, and he believes in the hope of the life everlasting.

True, we do not find in Clement the self-centered rather than the god-centered faith that characterized some Gnostics. We do not find the Pleroma, the Demiurge, the Aeons, or the archangels, but the number magic is there. This was the kind of thing that Philo loved. Philo understood Moses to say (in *Genesis*) that the six days of the Creation were symbolic of Order. Six was the number most suitable for productivity, for "if we start with 1, six is the perfect number being equal to the product of its factors as well as their sum (1, 2, 3), its half being 3, its third 2, and its sixth 1." Six is made up of male and female numbers: the odd 3 is male, and the even 2 is female; and 2 times 3 is six. Philo went into raptures over the virtues of 7 — which could not be factored; 7 was nature's favorite number: there were seven planets; human gestation occurred in seven months; there were seven internal organs in the human body; there were seven vowels, etc. This was why God rested on the seventh day.

Clement knew a lot about numbers that had escaped Philo. Abraham had won a great victory with his 318 servants. 318 was written in Greek: tau (300), iota (100), and eta (8). Tau (τ) was the sign of the Cross, and iota (ι) and eta (η) were the first two letters in "Jesus." Besides, 300 was 3 times the square of 10, and ten was the perfect number; everyone had known that since the time of Pythagoras. In addition, eight was the first cube, which represented equality in all directions. Shades of Nicomachus!

Origen, too, was not immune to Gnostic influence. He believed that the souls of men had existed in a previous state and that their imprisonment in material bodies was a punishment for sins which they had committed. The true Gnostic agreed with this, but also believed that by acquiring gnosis he would be redeemed and provided with the passwords which would let him ascend through various heavenly strata to his original habitat.

Gnosticism required a love of obscurities and complexities and a bent for mysticism that cannot have been commonly found in the ancient world. Ordinary people must have readily admitted that they could not make head nor tail of it, and did not want to. Even educated persons could not have been attracted to Gnosticism in great hordes. In fact, it is difficult to understand the concern of the Christians over Gnosticism. It can hardly have constituted a great menace.

The Church dealt with Gnosticism and other heresies by formulating orthodoxy and establishing the canon of the New Testament. Authority and discipline prevailed as they must in any warfare which is to have a successful outcome. In education also, Hellenism was brought to heel and Origen's plan of a Christian *paideia*[10] was considerably modified by his successors.

By the time of Basil it was possible to adopt an indulgent and patronizing tone. Everything we do, said Basil, is by way of preparation for the other life. It was perfectly permissible to hold converse with the ancients through their literature if one did not surrender to them the rudders of the mind. An agonist must undertake all sorts of preliminary training and exercise. Like bees among the flowers, the Christian could garner honey from the classics. "All Homer's poetry is an encomium of virtue," and Hesiod has similar merit. In other poetry and prose there was much good to be found. The Christian was a traveler on a long journey, and he would be prudent not to neglect supplies that might be found along the way.

FOOTNOTES

1. W. Jaeger, *Early Christianity and Greek Paideia,* Cambridge (Mass.) 1961, pp. 12-14.

2. Origen, *Commentary on John* 8 and Hippolytus, *Commentary on Kings* (frag.)

3. Eusebius, *Ecclesiastical History,* II, 17, 20.

4. Jaeger, *op. cit.,* p. 40.

5. Clement, *Stromata,* I.1.

6. *Ibid.,* I.2 and I.6.

7. *Ibid.,* I.9.

8. The theory of R. M. Grant, *Gnosticism and Early Christianity,* New York 1959. For a revised opinion, see his *Gnosticism,* New York 1961.

9. See the preliminary study of J. Doresse, *The Secret Books of the Egyptian Gnostics* (trans. by P. Mairet), New York 1960.

10. Jaeger, *op. cit.,* pp. 65-67.

Palinode

The dependent scholar! The great man's licensed friend! — if friend, not slave, is to be the word.

The Dependent Scholar

I never said that all drawers of salaries lived a degraded life....
Hippocleides doesn't care!

Apology for the Dependent Scholar

POMPEY THE GREAT, as Cicero was pained to discover, had no talent for politics. If we are to believe Aulus Gellius,[1] "Sulla's scholar" lacked even a rudimentary knowledge of civics: when he entered upon his first consulship with Crassus in the year 70 B.C. he had to solicit from Varro a handbook of parliamentary procedure so that he would know how to conduct the meetings of the senate. The profundity of Pompey's ignorance may have been a little less than this story suggests, but he cannot have lacked company; otherwise, Cicero's jejune sketch of the republican constitution in the *Laws* would have been pointless.

In the next one hundred and seventy-five years conditions showed little improvement. In a letter to Aristo[2] the younger Pliny complained that the return of liberty had found the senators ignorant and inexperienced, and he asked Aristo for advice on a matter of procedure. After a man of consular rank had been found dead, his freedmen were accused of murder. The evidence was not conclusive: it might have been a case of suicide, murder, or collusion. Pliny moved for acquittal; another senator, for banishment; and a third, for the death penalty. Pliny argues that there could not be a threefold division of the senate, that each proposal must be considered separately in the order in which it had been made. His view prevailed with the result that the senator advocating the death penalty abandoned his cause and sided with the faction demanding exile. Pliny's original motion for acquittal was thus defeated as his opponents joined forces, but the freedmen were only banished instead of being executed. Although it was all over and done with, Pliny still wondered whether he had been right on the parliamentary question.

A generation later Aulus Gellius found the authorities at variance over the question of whether a quaestor could be summoned to appear in the court of a praetor. An actual case of this kind had arisen, and many people argued that the praetor lacked the authority to arrest another magistrate. Gellius solved the problem by citing what he had just read in the twenty-first book of Varro's *Antiquitates Rerum Humanarum* in which it was stated that an official who lacked the imperium — a quaestor or an aedile, for example — might even be haled into court by a private citizen. This clinched it: the quaestor was promptly brought to trial.

Gellius also discovered that people were vague about the constitutional rights of colonies and municipalities. The citizens of many municipalities were agitating for a change of status; they seemed to think that they would be in a more advantageous position if their municipalities were raised to the rank of colonies. Hadrian, said Gellius, had already demonstrated the error of this view. *Municipes* were Roman citizens from free towns who enjoyed special rights and were bound by no Roman laws except through their own free choice. Those who lived in colonies, on the other hand, were merely transplanted Romans who must adhere to the laws and institutions of Rome. The real trouble was that through ignorance of their rights, the *municipes* had already forfeited many valuable privileges.

The vagueness of Pliny about his government proved something of a handicap when he went out to Bithynia to assume his governorship. His uncertainty contributed to his disinclination to make decisions or to take action without first consulting the emperor; this is quite plain in many of the letters in the tenth book of his correspondence. Aulus Gellius started out with very little knowledge of the constitution, but his antiquarian interests proved valuable: by reading Varro, Capito, Labeo, Sabinus, and others he picked up some information about governmental functions and procedures. It is significant that most of the little tidbits that he treasured as real finds were things that a well-informed citizen ought to have known as a matter of course. Clearly, the educational system was at fault.

Once, said Tacitus, Pliny, and Aulus Gellius,[3] the education of a Roman had included training in citizenship. In the good old days children had learned virtue and morality at home from their parents, and a boy got his first lessons in government by accompanying his father to the Forum and the Senate. When this primitive system was abandoned, nothing was provided to take its place. In the schools of grammatistic, grammar, and rhetoric, morality was not successfully inculcated, and the curriculum lacked anything approaching what we should call "civics" or "political science." Contrary to modern popular belief, the ancients seem to have learned very little about their political institutions by "doing."

However well-intentioned the Good Emperors might have been, they could hardly share the government with people who lacked the knowledge or will to govern themselves. The Senate consistently failed to take the initiative even when it had the opportunity. The subjects of the emperor were generally content, and some of them were quite eager to be his servants. In the end, it was the emperor who made the rules. He had to.

As the second century wears on, order seems to come out of chaos. The functions of governmental officials are defined by imperial constitutions and by the writings of the jurists. Long before the Theodosian Code of the fifth century, brief descriptions setting forth the duties of each office must have been made available in the bureaucracy. This is suggested by the passages from Ulpian and other jurists preserved in the *Digest* of Justinian. A government which was becoming increasingly complex and also better organized from the time of Hadrian onward could scarcely have operated efficiently in any other way.

The ability of Hadrian as an administrator is beyond question. People were amazed at his complete acquaintance with details of the budget, while his reforms and innovations in government were of the greatest importance.[4] Service or employment with the government became more and more desirable as the bureaucracy expanded. Appian, Suetonius, Chariton the novelist, and finally, Lucian, were to join the jurists in the imperial civil service.

Even before the second century, but very definitely in that period, there was a tendency to bring Greeks and others from the Roman East into the imperial service. Herodes Atticus was only one of several to serve as a provincial governor and attain even to the consulship. This policy of enlisting essentially non-Romans was not inspired by the mere sentiment of philhellenism; it accomplished the very useful purpose of securing the loyalty of influential persons in the eastern provinces and helped to promote a certain Romanization of the East.[5] C. Antius Aulus Julius Quadratus was employed as an imperial governor in Syria and three provinces of Asia Minor; he held the consulship twice (93 and 105 A.D.); he served as proconsul in Crete and Cyrene and crowned his long career with the proconsulship of Asia in 106 A.D. D. Julius Quadratus Bassus of Pergamum had an even more distinguished career which included many provincial governorships and a victory over Decebalus in the second Dacian war.

One of the important and fascinating developments in recent scholarship has been the discovery of a selection process[6] by means of which able young men of senatorial rank were identified and encouraged to embark on life-long careers in the service of the emperor. A preliminary selection was apparently made even before the aspirants took up their first posts in the vigintivirate. At this bottom rung of the ladder of the *cursus honorum,* those with potential military prowess were made *IIIviri monetales* or *IVviri viarum curandarum,* while others, who might be more useful in the civil arm or who might not be career men at all, were enrolled as *Xviri stlitibus iudicandis* or *IIIviri capitales.* This initial service was followed by a stint in the army in the capacity of *tribunus laticlavus* where the young men were carefully watched; some of those who failed to show promise were weeded out, but the able ones were pushed on to higher posts which would give experience in civil and military administration and further opportunities for evaluation. A really promising man would, with the emperor's *commendatio,* attain the praetorship at an early age; subsequently, he would be employed in high provincial and military posts for a period of many years. The system was not foolproof; politics or nepotism might intervene to retard or to speed up a man's career progress. Nevertheless, the selection principle was a good one and increases our respect for the Roman government.

The more closely one observes the imperial government, the more it seems to grow in stature. The mutterings of disgruntled senators and the anguished howls of "persecuted" philosophers, each one of whom fancied himself as a new Socrates, the victim of intolerance who would be vindicated by the judgement of posterity, should not divert our attention from an appreciation of the merits of the principate. A régime that brought order out of chaos, an organization whose efficiency grew with the passing of time until disaster struck in the third century, a state with a social conscience and a sense of public responsibility deserves only respect. The humanization of the law effected by the constitutions of the emperors and the labors of the jurists, the concern for public welfare reflected in the *alimenta* or in the provincial surveys of Hadrian, the aid to education – misguided though it may have been, or the refusal of Marcus Aurelius to approve a bonus to the soldiers because it would only come out of the blood of their parents and kinsmen[7] demonstrate the temper of the government. We must admire a Trajan who wrote: "Anonymous accusations must not be admitted in evidence against anyone, for this would introduce a most dangerous precedent not in keeping with the spirit of our age."[8] We also sympathize with a Marcus Aurelius who hated to get up in the morning.[9]

⊕

It was not a golden age, nor a silver age, nor even a happy one. It was just one portion of the past of which we are permitted something more than a glimpse. What do we find? Only what Ecclesiastes would have predicted:

All is vanity.... All the rivers run into the sea, yet the sea is not full....and there is no new thing under the sun.

We have emphasized too much, perhaps, the follies and foibles of the Pax Romana, and we have neglected to say that in no other age do people admit us so completely into their private lives. The papyri speak eloquently of the hopes and fears of the almost anonymous villagers of Karanis, Tebtunis, or Antinoopolis; petitions and letters reveal their troubles with unneighborly neighbors, their little family problems, the forced cheerfulness of homesick boys who have joined the navy to see the world. Inscriptions from all parts of the empire tell us of life and death in the microcosm of Cirta, Eburacum, or Pessinus. Aristocrats are no less frank than commoners. Gellius is ingenuous, to say the least. When the younger Pliny stops posturing and writes with real feeling about his family and friends or his life in the country, he ceases to be a puppet and becomes a human being. Sometimes he can even describe other people for us: his asthmatic uncle or grand old Verginius Rufus who might have been emperor and who broke his leg at eighty-four while rehearsing the speech intended to thank the emperor for his third consulship. At the very highest level, pomp and circumstance are stripped away in the warm, friendly correspondence of Fronto and Marcus Aurelius where genuine feeling often emerges victorious over the shallowness of rhetoric. Fronto's love of children was a deep and abiding thing. He writes to Marcus of the twins, Commodus and Antoninus, "I have seen your little chicks.... so like in features to you that nothing can be more like than the likeness."... or to his own son-in-law Victorinus: [10]

Daily tiffs indeed or disagreements I have with our little Victorinus or our little Fronto. While you never ask for any reward of anyone for act or speech, your little Fronto prattles no word more readily or more constantly than this *Da*. I on my part do my best to supply him with scraps of paper and little tablets, things which I wish him to want. Some signs, however, even of his grandfather's characteristics does he show. He is very fond of grapes.... he is also devoted to little birds.... I have often heard from those who were my tutors and masters that I had from my earliest infancy a passion for such things.

When all is said and done, we come back to Marcus Aurelius himself, who in the *Meditations* was often the least reserved of all his contemporaries. He found that it was not easy to be a "citizen of the world," for it was a world from which he derived little pleasure after becoming emperor. He was grateful to philosophy, he said, for having given him the strength to do his duty and to overcome his fear of death. Marcus also congratulated himself that he had escaped preoccupation with rhetoric, astrology, dialectic, and history — "and I did not fall into the hands of any sophist."[11]

Poor Marcus Aurelius! He missed all the fun.

FOOTNOTES

1. Aulus Gellius, *Attic Nights*, XIV, 7.

2. Pliny, *Letters*, VIII, 14.

3. Tacitus, *Dialogus*, 28; Pliny, *Letters*, VIII, 14; Aulus Gellius, *Attic Nights*, I, 23.

4. *Scriptores Historiae Augustae, Hadrian*, XX; F. Pringsheim, "The Legal Policy and Reforms of Hadrian," *Journal of Roman Studies*, XXIV (1934), pp. 141-153.

5. C. S. Walton, "Oriental Senators in the Service of Rome," *Journal of Roman Studies*, XIX (1929), pp. 38-66.

6. E. Birley, "Senators in the Emperors' Service," *Proceedings of the British Academy*, XXXIX (1953), pp. 197-214.

7. Cassius Dio, *Epitome*, LXXII, 10.

8. Pliny, *Letters*, X, 97.

9. Marcus Aurelius, *Meditations*, V, 1.

10. Reprinted by permission of the publishers from C. R. Haines, *Marcus Cornelius Fronto*, Cambridge, Mass.: Harvard University Press, 1919. The passage will be found in Vol. II, p. 173.

11. Marcus Aurelius, *Meditations*, I, 17.

Supplementary Notes

Chapter 1

● P. 9—The quotations are from *The Decline and Fall of the Roman Empire*, New York (Modern Library), n.d., Vol. I, p. 70 and *Greek Anthology, Sepulchral Epigrams*, no. 309. This quotation from the *Greek Anthology* and those from epigrams 118 and 489 are reprinted by permission of the publishers from *Greek Anthology*, Cambridge, Mass.: Harvard University Press.

For an excellent translation and an impressive commentary on Aristides, *Roman Oration*, see James H. Oliver, "The Ruling Power," *Transactions of the American Philosophical Society*, (new series) XLIII, part 4 (1953), pp. 869-1003.

Dio Chrysostom, a prominent orator in the period from Domitian to Trajan, came from Prusa in Asia Minor. The reference here is to his *Third Discourse*, 45.

Pliny the Younger, Latin orator and epistolographer, was a contemporary of Dio. The reference is to his *Letters*, III, 20.

Plutarch of Chaeronea (d. 120 A.D.), the author of the famous *Parallel Lives*, was also noted as a philosopher and essayist. His collected works are known as the *Moralia*. The reference here is *Precepts of Statecraft*, 824C.

● P. 10—Tacitus, a contemporary of Pliny the Younger, was a great historian and prominent as an orator. His view cited here may be found in the *Agricola*, 3.

Arrian, another contemporary, is best known for his history of Alexander the Great and his publication of the discourses of the philosopher Epictetus including a condensation of these discourses, the *Encheiridion*. The reference here is to the *Discourses of Epictetus*, III, 8, 10.

Dio's views on urbanization may be found in his *Seventh Discourse*, 109 ff. This is the well-known Euboean Discourse. See John Day, "The Value of Dio Chrysostom's Euboean Discourse for the Economic Historian," in *Studies in Roman Economic and Social History* (ed., P. R. Coleman-Norton), Princeton 1951, pp. 209-235.

● P. 11—On the monetary crisis, see S. Bolin, *State and Currency in the Roman Empire to 300 A.D.*, Stockholm 1958, p. 208 ff.; Cassius Dio, *Epitome*, 68, 2, 1 and 68, 14, 4; *Scriptores Historiae Augustae, Marcus Aurelius*, XVII.

For Bithynia, see Pliny, *Letters*, X, 17a, 23, 33, 37, 39, 70, and 90.

● P. 12—For Dio, see *Discourses*, nos. 32, 34, 38, 39, 40, 41, 42, 43, 45, 46, 47, etc.

● P. 13—See Pliny, *Letters*, IV, 20 and 25 for the behaviour of the Senate.

Florus, the author of an epitome of Roman history based on Livy, flourished during the reign of Hadrian. His remarks cited here will be found in his *Epitome of Roman History*, I, 1.

Chapter 2

● P. 17—The quotations are from Petronius, *Satyricon*, VII and Diogenes, *Lives of the Philosophers*, V, 18. Petronius, the ultimate patrician and arbiter of fashion at the court of Nero, is generally supposed to have been the author of the *Satyricon*. The first chapter of this work also contains some remarks on contemporary education. Diogenes Laertius seems to have lived in the early third century. Additional comments on education will be found in Book V, 20 of his work.

● P. 18—The principal authors drawn upon for the material in this chapter are:

Quintilian, *Institutes of Oratory*. A famous orator and teacher, Quintilian instructed Pliny the Younger, the children of Domitian, and many others. The pertinent passages in the *Institutes* are I, 1, 1-3, 16-19, 46, 73; II, 3, 5; 5, 21; 11; 19, 2; I, 2, 23; 2, 8; 3, 1; 3, 6; 4, 22; 6, 45; 8, 6; 9, 21; 10; 12, 17; X, 1, 20, 52, 81-82; 123; 2, 4-10; 3; 5, 2; XI, 2; XII, 2, 2; ll, 14-16.

Tacitus, *Dialogus* (Dialogue on Oratory), 2, 22, 23, 28, 29, 32, 33, 35.

Plutarch, *Education of Children*, 4-13; *How a Young Man Should Study Poetry*, 4, 36-37; *On Listening to Lectures*, 3, 7, ff., 48.

Seneca, *Epistles*, 33 and 76. Seneca, tutor of Nero and prominent in literature and philosophy, was an essayist, playwright, scientist, and literary stylist.

- P. 19—Vitruvius, a contemporary of Augustus, wrote on architecture. His educational ideas are expressed in I, 1-8 of his work, *On Architecture.*

- P. 20—On the worthlessness of anthologies, see Pliny, *Letters,* VII, 9 and Quintilian, *Institutes,* X, 1, 20.

- P. 21—See Lucian, *Rhetorician, passim.* Lucian, the great satirist, was one of the most talented authors of the second century. A good sampling for his low opinion of philosophers, mentioned below, may be found in the *Icaromenippus* or the *Sale of the Creeds.*
    Dio Chrysostom touches on education in his discourses. See, no. 4, 30 and 37; no. 11 *passim*; no. 13, 17; no. 18, 9, 11, and 14.

- P. 25—Sextus Empiricus, whose forte was dialectic, seems to have lived in the late second or early third century. In connection with the material of this chapter his works, *Against the Grammarians* and *Against the Rhetoricians* may be read. Sextus was critical of all educational practices of his day; his shotgun technique blasted both the contemporary and traditional approaches.

Chapter 3

- P. 29—The quotation is from the *Greek Anthology, Declamatory Epigrams,* no. 489.

- P. 31—The remarks of Sextus Empiricus may be found in his *Against the Professors,* I, 3, 12, and 13.
    For Dionysius Thrax, see G. Uhlig, *Dionysii Thracis Ars Grammatica,* Leipsig 1883; and for the grammarians, A. Hilgard, *Scholia in Dionysii Thracis Artem Grammaticam,* (Vol. III of *Grammatici Graeci*) Leipsig 1901.
    For rapid calculation 3 was often used instead of 22/7. Of course, the Greeks and Romans would have to say "three and one-seventh" since they had only one fraction whose numerator was more than 1; that was 2/3.

- P. 32—For Palaemon, see *Scholia on Juvenal,* VI, 452 and Suetonius, *On Grammarians,* 23.

- P. 33—On the schools of rhetoric, see Sextus Empiricus, *Against the Rhetoricians, passim* and Tacitus, *Dialogus,* 26.

● P. 34—These Greek themes and others are mentioned by Philo-stratus, *Lives of the Sophists.*

● P. 36—For the recommendations, see Quintilian, *Institutes,* I, 8; X, 65-105; Dio, *Eighteenth Discourse,* 6-13; Tacitus, *Dialogus,* 20 and 23; Longinus, *On the Sublime,* 12; Plutarch, *Comparison between Aris-tophanes and Menander.*

● P. 39—Householder's lists of school authors were compiled from his analyses of Dionysius Thrax, Sextus Empiricus, Quintilian, Statius, Dionysius of Halicarnassus, Dio, Theon, and Hermogenes. See House-holder, *op. cit.,* p. 56.

Chapter 4

● P. 49—The quotations are from the *Natural History,* Preface 15 of Pliny the Elder, uncle of Pliny the Younger. The elder Pliny perished in the eruption of Vesuvius in A.D. 79. For his work as a scholar, see footnote 1 of this chapter (page 66). The second quotation is from the *Attic Nights,* Preface 12 of Aulus Gellius (b. *circa* 130 A.D.). For further details regarding Aulus Gellius, see pp. 50-51.

For brief notices of the scholars here mentioned, see J. E. Sandys, *Short History of Classical Scholarship,* Cambridge 1915, pp. 60-64; 79-85.

Galen (b. 131 A.D.) was an exact contemporary of Aulus Gellius; for his work, see Chapter 7.

● P. 51—Valerius Maximus dedicated his books of historical anecdotes to the Emperor Tiberius.

● P. 52—The material discussed here will be found in Demetrius, *On Style,* II, 48, 51, 52, 68, 70, 75, 77, 80, 86, 94-99, 114, 124, and 127.

● P. 53—On Favorinus, see below p. 79 ff.

● P. 55—The material from Aulus Gellius, *Attic Nights,* will be found in II, 23; III, 1 and 3; IV, 15; X, 3; XI, 4; XII, 2; XVII, 10; XVIII, 5.

● P. 57—For Petronius, see the *Satyricon,* 1, 88, and 118. Also see Nettleship (footnote 10 to this chapter).

● P. 58—Six satires of the poet Persius (34-62 A.D.) survive. For this material, see the *First Satire.*

For Greek literary criticism, see Dio, *Discourses,* nos. 2, 11, 12, and 55; Plutarch, *How a Young Man Should Study Poetry;* Lucian, *Encomium on Demosthenes.*

● P. 59—Plutarch, *Comparison of Aristophanes and Menander;* Dio, *Fifty-second Discourse.*

● P. 61—See Longinus, *On the Sublime,* 14 and 33-36.

● P. 64—On Pliny, see *Natural History,* XXXIV, 2 and XXXV, 1.

The relevant passages in Philostratus (for pages 64 and 65) are *Imagines,* I, 4, 9, 23, and 30; II, 17 and 20. Reprinted by permission of the publishers from A. Fairbanks, *Philostratus,* Cambridge, Mass.: Harvard University Press, 1925.

Chapter 5

● P. 69—The quotations are from Lucian, *Demonax,* 28 and Philostratus, *Lives of the Sophists,* II, 12.

● P. 70—The quotations from Epictetus may be found in *Diatribes* (Discourses) III, 28, 5; I, 28, 10; III, 22, 51; III, 5; I, 29, 9 and *Encheiridion,* 29. The translator is W. A. Oldfather. The quotation from Seneca is from *On Providence,* 4-5.

Athenaeus, *Deipnosophistae,* I, 2. Athenaeus, the author of the *Banquet of the Sophists,* lived in Egypt in the third century. His work is more than a "glorified cook book," for it is a treasury of quotations from earlier authors, particularly of the Hellenistic period, whose works have not survived.

● P. 72—For Proteus (Peregrine) see Aulus Gellius, *Attic Nights,* VIII, 3; XII, 11; Philostratus, *Lives of the Sophists,* II, 1; and Lucian's *Peregrine.*

Seneca's *Apocolocyntosis* was a satire on his benefactor, the Emperor Claudius, composed just after Claudius' death. It was in the worst possible taste. *Apocolocyntosis* (pumpkinification) is a play on the word *apotheosis* (deification).

For Euphrates, see Pliny, *Letters,* I, 10; Epictetus, *Diatribes,* III, 15, 8; IV, 18, 17; Philostratus, *Life of Apollonius,* V, 27-33; Cassius Dio, *Epitome,* 69, 8.

● P. 73—For Musonius Rufus, see *Attic Nights*, IX, 2; XVI, 1; XVIII, 2; Dio Chrysostom, *Thirty-first Discourse*, 122, and many references in Epictetus. Also, M. P. Charlesworth, *Five Men*, Cambridge (Mass.) 1936.

    For Epictetus, see *Attic Nights*, I, 2; XVII, 9; XIX, 1. Epictetus, *Diatribes*, I, 4 and 29; II, 9 and 11; *Encheiridion*, 7 and 17.

● P. 75—Chrysippus was a famous Stoic and dialectician of the third century B.C. See Diogenes Laertius, *Lives of the Philosophers*, VII, 7.

    For Apuleius, the African rhetorician and author of the *Metamorphoses*, see below, p. 81.

    Aulus Gellius' reminiscences of student days may be found in *Attic Nights*, I, 26; VII, 16; XVII, 8 and 20; XVIII, 2 and 3.

● P. 76—See particularly, Philostratus, *Lives of the Sophists*, I, 22 and 25; II, 5, 6, and 10.

● P. 81—For Dio Chrysostom, see Philostratus, *op. cit.*, I, 7; II, 9, 12, and 31.

Chapter 6

● P. 83—The quotation is from Apuleius, *Metamorphoses*, X, 33.

    These remarks are found in Dio, *Seventy-fifth Discourse*, 9; *Digest*, I, 1; *Institutes*, I, 1; *Digest*, I, 10.

● P. 85—See Pliny, *Letters*, IV, 11 and II, 19.

● P. 86—See Tacitus, *Dialogus*, 6 ff.; 37 and 41.

    The material in Pliny, *Letters* is as follows: VI, 29; X, 3A and 3B; II, 11 and 12; VI, 29; III, 4 and 9; II, 11 and 14; III, 9; IV, 9 and 16; VI, 33.

● P. 88—For Regulus, see Pliny, *Letters*, I, 5 and 20; II, 20; IV, 2 and 7; VI, 2.

    The remarks of Quintilian may be found in *Institutes*, IV, *passim*; V, 13; VII, 1; XII, 3-8.

● P. 89—On this, see Tacitus, *Dialogus*, 38 ff.; Quintilian, *Institutes*, IV, 5; VII, 8 ff.; XII, 39; Pliny, *Letters*, IV, 29; V, 4, 9, and 13; VI, 2 5, 15, and 31.

● P. 96—See Gaius, *Institutes,* IV, especially 39 ff. as well as Jolowicz, *Historical Introduction,* p. 195 ff. and p. 205.

Chapter 7

● P. 101—The first quotation is from *Greek Anthology, Satirical Epigrams,* no. 118; the second, from Pliny the Elder, *Natural History,* XXIX, 8.

The story about Galen and Marcus is from Galen, *Prognosis,* XI.

On theriac, see Cassius Dio, *Epitome,* 72, 6; Aulus Gellius, *Attic Nights,* XVII, 16; Galen, *Antidotes,* I, 1.

The exchanges between Marcus Aurelius and Fronto may be found in S. A. Naber, *M. Cornelii Frontonis et M. Aurelii Imperatoris Epistulae,* Lipsiae 1867. The following list of pages in Naber together with the translations in Haines (footnote 1) shows the order of events:

NABER	HAINES
p. 252	I, p. 18
45	34
3	80
56	172
68	178
69	180
92	186
80	194
81	198
72	202
83	212
84	218
81	224
90	224
82	226
89	244
90	246
90	248
91	250
78	192
80	198
79	197

● P. 103—The examples of mortality here cited may be found in *Greek Anthology, Sepulchral Epigrams,* nos. 224, 323, 632, 308; see also, Fronto (Haines, *op. cit.,* I, p. 154); Pliny, *Letters,* IV, 21; Quintilian, *Institutes,* VI, 1-6.

● P. 104—See Pliny, *Natural History,* XXIX, 8; Juvenal, *Satires,* X, 209; Martial, *Epigrams,* VI, 53; VIII, 74; I, 30; *Greek Anthology, Satirical Epigrams,* no. 125.

● P. 105—For the schools of medicine, see Galen, *On the Medical Sects;* also Allbutt, *Greek Medicine in Rome.*

● P. 106—On the competition at Rome, see Galen, *On Prognosis,* IV and Epictetus, *Diatribes,* III, 33.

● P. 108—On hydrophobia, see Galen, *On the Sects,* VIII; Celsus, *De Medicina,* V, 27; Aurelianus (footnote 12), p. 387.

● P. 109—On Paralysis; Aurelianus, p. 565 and Aretaeus (footnote 11), pp. 307-8.

● P. 110—On tetanus: Aretaeus, pp. 246-249.

● P. 111—On dentistry: Aurelianus, p. 619; Celsus, *De Medicina,* VI 13.
   On burns: Celsus, *op. cit.,* V, 27.
   On classification of disease: Aurelianus, Book I, 3 and III, 5 Aretaeus, p. 478.

● P. 112—On gestation: Aulus Gellius, *Attic Nights,* III, 16 and X, 2 Pliny, *Natural History,* VII, 42; Justinian, *Digest,* V, 4, 3.

Chapter 8

● P. 117—The quotation is from Juvenal, *Satires,* VII, 105.

● P. 122—On the opinions of Dionysius, see *Letter to Pompeius* III-IV.

● P. 124—On Pliny, see *Letters,* IV, 16 and 20; VII, 33, IX, 27, V, 8

● P. 126—For Fronto as historian, see Haines, *Marcus Cornelius Fronto,* Vol. II, pp. 158, 194, and 196 (Naber 107, 131, and 202).

● P. 128—Herodian wrote a history that covered the period from Marcus Aurelius to 238 A.D. For an English translation, see E. C. Echols, *Herodian's History of the Roman Empire*, Berkeley 1961.

Chapter 9

● P. 131—The quotation is from Aelian, *Characteristics of Animals*, II, 30.

The material on pp. 131-132 will be found in Aelian, *op. cit.*, I, 2, 11, 12, 23, 24, 25, 49, and 53; II, 11, 23, 38, 45, and 46; III, 13; IV, 10; V, 10 and 47; VI, 31 and 58; VII, 2, 30, 43, and 44; IX, 50 and 55; X, 13; Pliny, *Natural History*, VIII, 1, 3, 5, 14, and 23; IX, 4, 8, 26, and 54; X, 5, 7, and 82; XI, 16 and 35; Seneca, *Natural Questions*, III, 2.

Aelian was an author of the third century who also compiled a set of historical anecdotes in the manner of Valerius Maximus. If anything, his history is inferior to his natural history.

● P. 134—On Frontinus, see Pliny, *Letters*, IV, 8 and IX, 19; Frontinus, *De Aquis*, I, 24 ff. and II, 87; also C. Herschel, *Frontinus and the Water Supply of the City of Rome*, New York 1913, especially p. 61 and 239.

● P. 135—On novelties, see Pliny, *Natural History*, VII, 21; XIX, 4; XXV, 4; Aulus Gellius, *Attic Nights*, X, 12, 10; XV, 1, 6; Heron, *Dioptra*, 34; *Deipnosophistae*, I, 34; Virtuvius, *On Architecture*, X, 8; Suetonius, *Vespasian*, XVIII.

● P. 136—Optics and sound: Vitruvius, *On Architecture*, V, 3; Diogenes Laertius, *Lives of the Philosophers*, VII, 158; Pliny, *Natural History*, II, 55; Seneca, *Natural Questions*, I, 16; Aulus Gellius, *Attic Nights*, XVI, 18; G. L. Huxley, *Anthemius of Tralles in Greek, Roman, and Byzantine Monographs*, no. 1 (1959).

● P. 137—Shape of the earth: Ptolemy, *Optics*, V; Pliny, *Natural History*, II, 1-3; 65-66; Diogenes Laertius, *Lives of the Philosophers*, VII, 140; X, 74 ff.; Aulus Gellius, *Attic Nights*, II, 22, 3.

Size of the earth: Pliny, *Natural History*, II, 112; Strabo, *Geography*, II, 12; for Cleomedes and Poseidonius, see M. R. Cohen and I. E. Drabkin, *Source Book in Greek Science*, New York 1948, p. 153.

● P. 140 ff.—On earthquakes: Seneca, *Natural Questions*, VI, 3-20; Strabo, *Geography*, I, 3, 17; Herodotus, VII, 129; Diodorus, *Universal*

History, I, 81, 5 and II, 30, 5; Pliny, *Natural History*, II, 81; Ammianus, XVII, 7, 11; Diogenes Laertius, *Lives of the Philosophers*, VII, 154 and X, 154.

● P. 143—In Ptolemy, *Tetrabiblos*, see I, 2, 4, 5, and 6; II, 2 and 3.

Chapter 10

● P. 147—The quotations are from C. A. Baynes, *A Coptic Gnostic Treatise*, Cambridge 1933, p. 65; St. Ignatius, *To the Philadelphians*, 3; and Origen, *Against Celsus*, IX.

● P. 148—For the apologists, see Eusebius, *Ecclesiastical History*, IV, 3 ff. Among the apologies are the *Letter to Diognetus*, possibly the work of Quadratus addressed to Hadrian, the two apologies of Justin which date from the reign of Antoninus, the work of Athenagoras addressed to Marcus Aurelius and Commodus, that of Aristides (reign of Hadrian), and the Theophilus, *To Autolycus* (reign of Marcus Aurelius).

For Porphyry, see Eusebius, *Ecclesiastical History*, VI, 19, 4ff. A convenient translation of Tatian's *Address to the Greeks* may be found in *Ante-Nicene Christian Library*, III, Edinburgh 1867; for Hippolytus, *Refutation of all Heresies*, see Vol. VI of the same series (1868).

● P. 151—For the *Octavius* of Minucius Felix, see the translation by J. H. Freese in Series II (Latin Texts), *Translations of Christian Literature*, London 1938.

On allegorical interpretation, see Clement, *Stromata*, V, 4 ff.

● P. 152—For the life of Origen, see Eusebius, *Ecclesiastical History*, VI, 6 ff.

● P. 153—The oration of Gregory addressed to Origen may be found in the *Ante-Nicene Fathers*, VI, New York 1888. The exchange between Africanus and Origen may be found in *Ante-Nicene Christian Library*, X, Edinburgh 1869.

● P. 154—For the *Diatessaron*, see *Ante-Nicene Fathers*, IX, New York 1896.

The stand taken by Irenaeus and Tertullian is best stated in Irenaeus, *Against Heresies*, I, 10 and Tertullian, *Prescription against Heretics*, VII-XIII.

On gnosticism, see Baynes, *op. cit.*; Doresse, footnote 9; Grant, footnote 8; F. L. Cross, ed., *The Jung Codex*, London 1955; G. Quispel, *Gnosis als Weltreligion*, Zürich 1951. For a recent and very good discussion, see R. M. Grant, *Gnosticism*, New York 1961. For Clement and gnosticism, see *Stromata*, VI, 7 ff.

● P. 156—The examples taken from Philo may be found in his *On the Creation*, III and his *Allegorical Interpretation of Genesis*, I, 4. See also Clement, *Stromata*, VI, 11.

● P. 157—Basil's *Address to Young Men* is most conveniently found in *Saint Basil: The Letters*, trans. By R. J. Deferrari, IV (Loeb Classical Library), London and Cambridge (Mass.) 1934.

Palinode

● P. 159—The quotations are from Lucian, *The Dependent Scholar*, 1 and his *Apology for the Dependent Scholar*, 12 and 15.

The passages from Aulus Gellius, *Attic Nights*, may be found in XIII, 13 and XVI, 13.

● P. 161—For C. Antius Aulus Julius Quadratus, see *Prosopographia Imperii Romani*, no. 338; for a convenient summary of the career of C. Julius Quadratus Bassus, see R. K. Sherk, *The Legates of Galatia from Augustus to Diocletian*, Baltimore 1951, pp. 56-58.

Texts and Translations

THE READER who does not readily use Greek or Latin will perhaps be interested to know that most of the ancient authorities cited in the footnotes are available in translation in the Loeb Classical Library series. Where the Loeb is not complete, the older Bohn Classical Library may often be used as, for example, in the case of Pliny's *Natural History*. The following authors pertinent to this study are now in the Loeb, either in full or in part:

Aelian	Josephus
Alciphron	Juvenal
Ammianus Marcellinus	Livy
Apostolic Fathers	Longinus
Appian	Lucan
Apuleius	Lucian
Arrian	Martial
Athenaeus	Marcus Aurelius
St. Basil	Oppian
Cassius Dio	Pausanian
Celsus	Persius
Cicero	Petronius
Clement of Alexandria	Philo
Demetrius of Tarsus	Philostratus
Dio Chrysostom	Pliny the Elder
Diodorus Siculus	Pliny the Younger
Diogenes Laertius	Plutarch
Dionysius of Halicarnassus	Polybius
Epictetus	Ptolemy (Tetrabiblos)
Eunapius	Quintilian
Eusebius	Sallust
Florus	Scriptores Historiae Augustae
Fronto	Seneca
Frontinus	Sextus Empiricus
Galen	Statius
Greek Anthology	Strabo
Greek Mathematical Texts	Suetonius
Hesiod	Tacitus
Herodotus	Thucydides
Homer	Vitruvius

There are several translations of Ptolemy's *Almagest* and *Geography*. Translations of Aurelianus, Nicomachus, Heron, and Aretaeus are mentioned in the footnotes. The *Apologia* and *Florida* of Apuleius were translated by H. E. Butler (Oxford 1909). Herodian has recently been translated by E. C. Echols (Berkeley 1961). Much of Galen not translated into English may be found in the French version of C. Daremberg (see Bibliography), but some of his essays have never been translated into a modern language. I do not recall any translation of the *Panegyricus* of the younger Pliny or of the work of Polyaenus on stratagems, but the texts may be found in the Teubner series. Among other collections of texts (generally untranslated) might be listed:

Anecdota Graeca (ed. J. A. Cramer), Oxford 1837. *Rhetores Graeci* (ed. L. Spengel) Leipzig 1853-56. *Rhetores Latini Minores* (ed. K. Helm), Leipzig 1863. *Grammatici Graeci* (ed. A. Hilgard), Leipzig 1891. *Claudii Galeni Pergameni Scripta Minora* (Kühn), Leipzig 1891.

For the Christian authors, translations of most works can be found in the *Ante-Nicene Christian Library* or the *Ante-Nicene Fathers*; more recent series are the *Library of Christian Classics* and the *Fathers of the Church*.

Bibliography

Allbutt, T. C., *Greek Medicine in Rome,* London 1921.

Arnim, H. von, *Leben und Werke des Dio von Prusa,* Berlin 1898.

Arnold, E. V., *Roman Stoicism,* Cambridge 1911.

Ashburner, W., *Rhodian Sea Law,* Oxford 1909.

Ashby, T., *Aqueducts of Ancient Rome,* Oxford 1935.

Atkins, J. W. H., *Literary Criticism in Antiquity,* 2 vols., Cambridge 1934.

Baynes, C. A., *A Coptic Gnostic Treatise,* Cambridge 1933.

Berger, A., *Encyclopedic Dictionary of Roman Law,* Philadelphia 1953.

Birley, E., "Senators in the Emperors' Service," *Proceedings of the British Academy,* XXXIX (1953), pp. 197-214.

Blake, W. E., *Chaireas and Callirrhoe,* Oxford 1938.

Bolin, S., *State and Currency in the Roman Empire to 300 A.D.,* Stockholm 1958.

Bonner, S. F., *Literary Treatises of Dionysius of Halicarnassus,* Cambridge 1939.

——————, *Roman Declamation,* Liverpool 1949.

Boulanger, A., *Aelius Aristide,* Paris 1923.

Brock, A. J., *Greek Medicine,* London 1929.

Bryant, E. E., *Reign of Antoninus Pius,* Cambridge 1895.

Burton, H. E., *Discovery of the Ancient World,* Cambridge (Mass.) 1932.

Cambridge Ancient History, vols. X-XI, Cambridge 1934-36.

Capes, W. W., *University Life in Ancient Athens,* New York 1877.

Carcopino, J., *Daily Life in Ancient Rome,* New Haven 1941.

Charlesworth, M. P., *Five Men,* Cambridge (Mass.) 1936.

——————, *Roman Empire,* New York 1951.

Cooper, L., *An Aristotelian Theory of Comedy,* New York 1922.

Cramer, F. H., *Astrology in Roman Law and Politics,* Philadelphia 1954.

Crook, J., *Consilium Principis,* Cambridge 1955.

180 The Silver-Plated Age

Daremberg, C., *Oeuvres anatomiques, physiologiques et médicales de Galien*, 2 vols., Paris 1854.

Della Corte, F., *Suetonio, eques romanus*, Milan 1958.

Denniston, J. D., *Greek Literary Criticism*, London 1924.

Dill, S., *Roman Society from Nero to Marcus Aurelius*, London 1905.

Diller, A., "Ancient Measurements of the Earth," *Isis* 40 (1949), pp. 6-9.

D'Ooge, M. L., *Nichomachus of Gerasa*, New York 1926.

Doresse, J., *The Secret Books of the Egyptian Gnostics*, New York 1960.

Drabkin, I. E., "Poseidonius and the Circumference of the Earth," *Isis* 34 (1943), pp. 509-512.

——————, and Cohen, M.R., *Source Book in Greek Science*, New York 1948.

——————, *Caelius Aurelianus*, Chicago 1950.

Drachmann, A. G., "Ktesitius, Philon, and Heron," *Acta historica scientiorum naturalium et medicinalum*, IV (1948).

Dudley, D. R., *History of Cynicism*, London 1937.

Duff, J. W., *Literary History of Rome in the Silver Age*, (rev.) London 1959.

Dupuoy, E., *Médicine et moeurs de l'ancienne Rome*, Paris 1892.

Edmond, W. A., *Suasoriae of Seneca the Elder*, Cambridge 1928.

Farquharson, A. S. L., *Marcus Aurelius*, Oxford 1951.

Farrington, B., *Greek Science*, 2 vols., London 1949.

Frank, T., ed., *Economic Survey of Ancient Rome*, 5 vols., Baltimore 1933-40.

Gibbon, E., *Decline and Fall of the Roman Empire*, 7 vols., London 1896-1900 (ed. J. B. Bury).

Grant, R. M., *Gnosticism and Early Christianity*, New York 1959.

——————, *Gnosticism*, New York 1961.

Gwynn, J., *Roman Education*, Oxford 1926.

Hadas, M., *History of Greek Literature*, New York 1950.

——————, *History of Latin Literature*, New York 1952.

——————, *Stoic Philosophy of Seneca*, New York 1958.

Hamberg, P. G., *Studies in Roman Imperial Art*, Copenhagen 1945.

Hammond, M., *The Antonine Monarchy*, Rome 1959.

Henderson, B. W., *Life and Principate of the Emperor Hadrian*, London 1923.

Householder, F. W., *Literary Quotation and Allusion in Lucian*, New York 1941.

Jaeger, W., *Early Christianity and Greek Paideia*, Cambridge (Mass.) 1961.

Jolowicz, H. F., *Historical Introduction to the Study of Roman Law*, Cambridge 1952.

Jones, A. H. M., "Roman Civil Service," *Journal of Roman Studies* XXXIX (1949), pp. 38-55.

Jones, R. M., *Platonism of Plutarch*, Menasha 1916.

Jones, W. H. S., *Medical Writings of the Anonymous Londiniensis*, Cambridge 1947.

Lacey, R. H., *Equestrian Officials of Trajan and Hadrian*, Princeton 1917.

Laistner, M. L. W., *Greater Roman Historians*, Berkeley 1947.

Lepper, F. A., *Trajan's Parthian War*, Oxford 1948.

Lutz, C. E., "Musonius Rufus, the Roman Socrates," *Yale Classical Studies* 10 (1947), pp. 3-147.

Marrous, H.–I., *History of Education in Antiquity*, London 1956.

Moore, F. G., "Three Canal Projects, Roman and Byzantine," *American Journal of Archaeology* 44 (1950), pp. 97-111.

Musurillo, H. A., *Acts of the Pagan Martyrs*, Oxford 1954.

Nettleship, H., *Lectures and Essays*, (2nd series), Oxford 1895.

Nock, A. D., *Conversion*, London 1933.

Oldfather, W. A., *Greek Literary Texts from Greco-Roman Egypt*, Madison 1923.

Oliver, J. H., *The Ruling Power*, Philadelphia 1953.

Orgeval, B. d'., *L'empereur Hadrien*, Paris 1950.

Pack, R., *Greek and Roman Literary Texts from Greco-Roman Egypt*, Ann Arbor 1952.

Parks, E. P., *Roman Rhetorical Schools as a Preparation for the Courts under the Early Empire*, Baltimore 1945.

Pringsheim, F., "The Legal Policy and Reforms of Hadrian," *Journal of Roman Studies* XXIV (1934), pp. 141-153.

Roberts, W. R., *Dionysius of Halicarnassus: The Three Literary Letters*, Cambridge 1901.

——————————, *Dionysius of Halicarnassus on Literary Composition*, London 1910.

Sambursky, S., "On some References to Experience in Stoic Physics," *Isis* 49 (1958), pp. 331-335.

Sandys, J. E., *History of Classical Scholarship*, Vol. I, Cambridge 1903.

Sarton, G., *Galen of Pergamum*, Lawrence 1954.

——————, *History of Science*, Cambridge (Mass.) 1952.

Singer, C., *History of Technology*, Vol. II, Oxford 1956.

Schulz, O., *History of Roman Legal Science*, Oxford 1946.

Sellers, E., *The Elder Pliny's Chapters on the History of Art*, London 1896.

Sherk, R. K., *The Legates of Galatia from Augustus to Diocletian*, Baltimore 1951.

Stahl, W. H., "The Greek Heliocentric Theory and its Abandonment," *Transactions of the American Philological Association* 76 (1945), pp. 321-332.

Starr, C. G., *Civilization and the Caesars*, Ithaca 1954.

Syme, R., *Tacitus*, 2 vols., Oxford 1958.

Thomson, J. O., *History of Ancient Geography*, Cambridge 1934.

Toynbee, J. M. C., *The Hadrianic School*, Cambridge 1934.

Walden, J., *Universities of Ancient Greece*, London 1913.

Walton, C. S., "Oriental Senators in the Service of Rome," *Journal of Roman Studies* XIX (1929), pp. 38-66.

Walton, F. R., "Religious Thought in the Age of Hadrian," *Numen* 4 (1957), pp. 165-170.

Westaway, K. M., *Educational Theory of Plutarch*, London 1922.

Wilkins, A. S., *Roman Education*, Cambridge 1905.

Woodcroft, B., *Pneumatics of Hero of Alexandria*, London 1851.

Zeller, E., *History of Eclecticism in Greek Philosophy*, London 1883.

Zulueta, F. de, *Institutes of Gaius*, 2 vols., Oxford 1946.

Index

NOTES